Understandings of Prayer

BOOKS BY PERRY LEFEVRE
Published by The Westminster Press

Understandings of Prayer
Understandings of Man

Understandings of Prayer

by

PERRY LeFEVRE

THE WESTMINSTER PRESS
Philadelphia

Copyright © 1981 The Westminster Press

BOOK DESIGN BY DOROTHY ALDEN SMITH

Acknowledgment is made to the following publishers for permission to use copyrighted materials:

The Crossroad Publishing Co., for quotations from *Christian at the Crossroads,* by Karl Rahner. English translation © Search Press Limited 1975.

Harcourt Brace Jovanovich, Inc., and Curtis Brown, Ltd., for quotations from *Letters to Malcolm: Chiefly on Prayer,* by C. S. Lewis, © 1963, 1964 by the Estate of C. S. Lewis and/or C. S. Lewis.

Harper & Row, Publishers, Inc., for quotations from *I Knew Dietrich Bonhoeffer,* edited by Wolf-Dieter Zimmermann and Ronald Gregor Smith. Copyright © 1966 in the English translation by Wm. Collins Sons & Co., Ltd., London, and Harper & Row, Publishers, Inc., New York.

First edition

Published by The Westminster Press®
Philadelphia, Pennsylvania

PRINTED IN THE UNITED STATES OF AMERICA
9 8 7 6 5 4 3 2 1

Library of Congress Cataloging in Publication Data

LeFevre, Perry D.
    Understandings of prayer.

    Includes bibliographical references.
    1. Prayer—History—20th century. I. Title.
BV207.L44   248.3'2'0904   81-11622
    ISBN 0-664-24382-7   AACR2

Contents

Foreword

THE STUDIES of major twentieth-century theologies of prayer included in this book grew directly out of my teaching. Contemporary students, like many others in the recent past, have become deeply interested in prayer and meditation. Many books have been written telling their readers how to pray or how to meditate, but few have given attention to the underlying theological assumptions or to the theological questions involved in the practice of prayer or meditation. None has studied what the significant theologians of our time have had to say about prayer.

The present work attempts to look at the interpretations of the meaning of prayer offered by some major theologians or, in the cases of Thomas Merton and C. S. Lewis, at what two of the most popular writers on prayer and the spiritual life have understood to be their theological grounding. Several criteria have governed the selection of the figures to be presented. First, the writer should be both important and representative of a major theological option in the twentieth century. Second, the theologian should have written enough about the meaning of prayer and its theological understanding to have made a substantial contribution to the theology of prayer. In addition I have made a conscious decision to include Catholic, Protestant, and Jewish perspectives.

The popular ways of characterizing theologians—

e.g., neo-orthodox, empirical process, orthodox, mystic —are no doubt inaccurate, but they convey enough of the truth about the general stance of the theologian to be used as shorthand for the general position represented. Nevertheless, my intent is not to label the thinkers we shall be discussing. Rather, it is to help readers clarify their own thinking about the meaning of prayer and to point to the critical importance of prayer in living religion. Properly understood, prayer is both the center and heart of all religion, and the theological understanding of prayer may be the very center and heart of theology.

PERRY LEFEVRE

1
Historical Background

SUBJECTIVITY, concern, commitment, and faith are marks of living religion. Undoubtedly there are levels of "existentiality" in the religious life, but a philosophical world view, a way of understanding the world and of looking at life from a relatively detached point of view, is not yet living religion. A world view that sees reality as both meaningful and friendly comes closer, but living religion goes still farther. It senses a responsiveness in the reality that transcends the human. The friendliness is somehow "friend." The "Other" is not only friendly, not only worthy of commitment; the "Other" responds. However this Other is conceived, it is the awareness of this responsiveness which is at the heart of faith and of living religion and which makes it possible to understand what Luther meant when he said that faith is prayer and nothing but prayer.

More than fifty years ago the theologian Fernand Ménégoz warned of the crisis in religious life and in theology.[1] He thought that a theology which could neither justify nor give a constructive interpretation to the possibility and meaning of prayer was in a state of near-collapse. If prayer disappeared, so did living religion. He rejected the nineteenth-century theologies of prayer and looked to the emerging theology of Karl Barth as an answer to the crisis. Our intention in this book is to study not only Karl Barth's theology of prayer but other interpretations as well. Are the theologies of prayer in our day capable of sustaining living religion in the face of the kind of intellectual and social issues confronting faith in an increasingly secularized world? Paradoxically perhaps, we must ask whether they are capable of critically nurturing the renaissance of prayer and meditation that is so apparent in contemporary culture.

To understand these twentieth-century theologies of prayer we need to look at the way in which prayer was interpreted by those nineteenth-century thinkers who shaped the context out of which twentieth-century thought emerged and against which it has rebelled. But we must begin even earlier, with the thought of Immanuel Kant (1724–1804), whose philosophy was "decisive for the theology of the nineteenth century."[2]

IMMANUEL KANT

Immanuel Kant both affirms the Enlightenment's confidence in human reason (we need not and cannot any longer depend on authority or revelation) and establishes its limits (we cannot have *knowledge* of any reality transcending the phenomenal world). Kant believes that theoretical reason cannot reach beyond the objectified world to God, and therefore both natural theology and traditional metaphysics must be abandoned. There is, however, another possibility of access to that which transcends the phenomenal world. What Kant calls practical reason—reason in action—involves the sense of ought or obligation through which we experience the unconditional. The moral imperative presupposes human freedom and a highest good or "God" as its ground. Unless there is a guarantor of the ultimate validity and continuing possibility of pursuing virtue, the sense of obligation could have no objective reality.

Kant's path to God and his resulting conception of the relation between God and man is decisive for his view of prayer. The locus of prayer is exclusively in the dimension of moral obligation. The true service to God is a moral one. It lies in the *disposition* to obedience to all true duties as divine commands.[3] The "service of the heart," not visible action, is what is critical. A disposition dedicated to the Kingdom of God is the first requirement. For Kant this does not mean that visible actions are unimportant. The invisible needs to be represented by the visible. There are four visible actions that are related to this inward disposition dedicated to the Kingdom of God. *Prayer* serves to establish the desired goodness in ourselves. *Churchgoing* spreads it abroad. *Baptism* propagates it by receiving new members into the fellowship. *Communion* maintains this fellowship.

The central human task is to be morally responsible. To pray in order to please God is "fetish faith."[4] To pray, to ask for God's help, thinking that we can influence God is illusory. Such prayer

is no more than a stated wish directed to a Being who needs no such information regarding the inner disposition of the wisher; therefore nothing is accomplished by it, and it discharges none of the duties to which, as commands of God, we are obligated; hence God is not really served.[5]

We do not have to state the wish, nor do we have to address God, but we do have to *have* the wish, to have the disposition in all our actions to "perform these as though they were being executed in the service of God."[6] This is the spirit of prayer which can and should be present in us without ceasing. If we pray, in the sense of uttering words, these can have no bearing on God. If speaking does anything, Kant says, it may "quicken our disposition."[7] Whether this is desirable or not depends on the individual's need. Prayer under such circumstances, though ostensibly speaking with God, is really a way of working upon oneself. One is quickening one's disposition by means of the idea of God.

Kant believes his own views are consonant with
Jesus' teaching in the Lord's Prayer. He writes:

One finds in it nothing but the resolution to good life—conduct which, taken with the consciousness of our frailty, carries with it the persistent desire to be a worthy member in
the kingdom of God. Hence it contains no actual request for
something which God in His wisdom might well refuse us.[8]

Only a prayer arising in the moral disposition, that is,
animated solely by the idea of God, can be prayed with
faith. Only such prayer provides assurance that it will
be heard. Behind Kant's interpretation of prayer lies
not only his understanding of the way in which man
comes to know God through practical reason but also
his assumptions about the limitations of man and the
reality of God. On the one hand, because of his own
finiteness man cannot know what God knows. Man cannot know what God's view of the Good is in all its
fullness and richness. On the other hand, God is Absolute in his being. He is eternal, unchanging, omniscient,
unable to be influenced. He stands above and beyond
the causal process as we know it. It would be presump-
tuous, Kant thinks, to believe that God could be di-
verted to our present advantage from the plan of his
wisdom. Kant's view of God is not simply an abstract
metaphysical idea. For him it is a view demanded by
the concreteness of man's moral experience. If faith
grounded in moral obligation is to be genuinely possible, then God is a being with this kind of perfection. For
moral obligation to be genuine we must put our trust
in "a being who governs the world justly and benefi-
cently, with the power and wisdom to order it as is
best." In his third critique Kant speaks of faith as that
kind of trust:

Faith (absolutely so-called) is trust in the attainment of a
design, the promotion of which is a duty, but the possibility
of the fulfillment of which is not to be comprehended by us.

Or again:

Faith, then, denotes trust in God that he will supply our deficiency in things beyond our power, provided we have done all within our power.[9]

We can only place an absolute trust in God if God possesses these attributes, and human finitude together with such absolute trust, Kant thinks, makes it necessary to conceive of prayer as he does.

FRIEDRICH SCHLEIERMACHER

Friedrich Schleiermacher (1768–1834) was the father of modern Protestant theology. For him religion is neither theoretical knowledge nor moral obedience, both of which presuppose a disjunction between subject and object and therefore between man and God. The gap between the phenomenal and the noumenal (the objective world and that which transcends or stands behind it) is overcome in Schleiermacher by what he calls feeling. Feeling is not emotion, though it may include emotion. Rather, it is direct, immediate awareness. The foundation of religion is the feeling of absolute dependence. God is the "whence" of that feeling. On the one hand, the feeling of absolute dependence points to that on which we depend for our very being. On the other, it points to that on which we depend for our fulfillment as *human* beings. Both senses of dependence are present in Christianity. Such a conception of the nature of religion, grounded in the feeling of absolute dependence, led to a conception of God and God's relation to the world that does not give prayer an essentially different role than that which Kant gave it. If God is the kind of reality on whom man is absolutely dependent for his being and his well-being, this meant that in some ultimate sense man neither could nor needed to try to influence God. Every-

thing is finally "in God's hands," and therefore prayer
must be understood in some other fashion than that of
trying to bring about changes in God, or in God's attitude toward man, or in the world of persons and events.

For Schleiermacher the norm for prayer is the Kingdom of God. The object of prayer is to be in agreement
"with the order according to which Christ rules his
church, so that the person who prays may as such be
regarded as a true and acceptable representative of
Christ."[10] Such prayer can look for fulfillment, can be
sure of being answered, as can no other prayer except
to the degree that it can be harmonized with that norm.

Schleiermacher relates the understanding of Christian prayer to his understanding of the church. Since
the church knows that its actions in the world, its
achievements and its failures, are not solely the result
of its own strength, its reaction to past or present success or failure is either thanksgiving or resignation.
"But for that which still remains undecided it becomes
prayer—i.e., the inner combination with the God-con-
sciousness of a wish for full success."[11] Ideally, the
church could refrain from wishing altogether, for it
could hold "fast exclusively to the irrefragable certainty
of ultimate success."[12] But individual human beings are
not like this. They anticipate, imagine, and hope in
relation to the future, and combined with God-con-
sciousness their thoughts become prayer. Schleiermacher thinks that here the church's judgment should
be relied on to overcome the distortions of individual
wishing and praying. The church's judgment is more
likely to bring the prayer of its members into congru-
ence with "whatever may be necessary for the increase
and progress of the Kingdom of God."[13] This is what it
means to pray "in the name of Jesus." It is to bring the
objects of prayer "into agreement with the order by
which Christ rules His Church."[14] Schleiermacher
trusts the self-consciousness of the church as a whole to
be able to do this. When it does function in this fashion

such prayer "cannot but be fulfilled."[15] The further implication is that any other kind of prayer cannot be fulfilled.

Schleiermacher recognizes that this conclusion will create a problem for many. People will object that such a view makes "the whole doctrine of the hearing of prayer a delusion."[16] These objections presuppose that we "can exert an influence on God," whereas Schleiermacher's "basal presupposition is that there can be no relation of interaction between creature and Creator."[17] Prayer that assumes the opposite is a lapse into magic, says Schleiermacher. He thinks that those who support such a view by pointing to the "promises of Christ" are mistaken. Christ's promise that faith is the only condition of prayer's being heard means not faith that the prayer will be heard, but faith in Christ himself, "faith in the imperishable and supreme value of the Kingdom of God He was founding."[18] Schleiermacher addresses this issue in some detail both in his sermons and in *The Christian Faith*.

In a sermon entitled "The Power of Prayer," on the text Matt. 26:36–46, Schleiermacher describes prayer as the joining of the thought of God with every other thought of any importance to us, and he calls this the essence of true religion. "To be a religious man and to pray are really one and the same thing." He describes the benefits of prayer:

If our joys have often remained innocent, while others strayed into the ways of sin; if our judgments have been mixed with gentleness and modesty, where pride and arrogance might most easily have gained the day; if we have been guarded from the evil which the judgment of many all too willingly excuses; then we owe this beneficent protection to the power of prayer.[19]

But does prayer have another kind of power? Can prayer lead to the fulfillment of our wishes? Do our prayers help to change "things" that might have been otherwise? Schleiermacher turns to the example of

Jesus. Even Jesus' petitions in Gethsemane were not granted. Schleiermacher's conclusion: "This at least is certain, that where His prayer could not prevail, neither will ours succeed."[20] Yet petitionary prayer has value and power, and we certainly have the privilege of bringing our wishes about the more important concerns of our lives before God. Indeed we ought always to speak them when our heart is moved to do so, for this is a means of allaying our disquietude even as it was for Jesus. Does this mean that our wishes will be granted? No. God's plan is set and "sooner will heaven and earth pass away than the slightest tittle be changed of what has been decreed in the counsels of the Most High."[21] If we cannot bend his will, if we cannot change the unchangeable, then "what remains to us but to bring our will into accord with His?"[22] After all, Schleiermacher asks, what is human foresight into consequences and connections of events related to our own well-being compared with that of a God who "knows the best and the whole."[23] Moreover, God is not only wise but kind. We can trust Him, for "whatever befalls us, good must come of it."[24]

From this general position Schleiermacher draws certain consequences. *(a)* "If nothing is changed on account of our prayers in the course of things ordained by God, we must not attach any special value to occasional *apparent* answers that we may receive [italics mine]." *(b)* "There is no true prayer . . . but the prayer we offer when we have the living thought of God accompanying, purifying and sanctifying all our other thoughts, feelings and purposes." All other forms of prayer must resolve themselves into such prayer. *(c)* "It seems to me a mark of greater and more genuine piety when this entreating kind of prayer is only seldom used by us." Prayer in which we try to make God's power favorable to us is "dictated by a weak heart" and rests on a "defective idea of God." Those who persist in this kind of prayer are "still very far from the spirit of true godly fear." If, says Schleiermacher, you are overtaken by such an occasion, "then entreat until the prayer makes you forget entreaty."[25] He then goes on to describe the genuine benefits of petitionary prayer by referring to Jesus' own experience at prayer in Gethsemane:

> Consider with me what passed, on that occasion, in His mind. He began with the definite wish that His sufferings might pass away from Him; but as soon as He fixed His thought on His Father in heaven to whom He prayed, this wish was at once qualified by the humble, "if it be possible." When from the sleeping disciples, the sight of whom must have still more disheartened Him and added fresh bitterness to His sense of desertion, He returned to prayer, He already bent His own wish before the thought that the will of the Father might be something different. To reconcile Himself to this, and willingly to consent to it, was now His chief object; nor would He have wished that the will of God should not be done, had He been able by that means to gain all that the world could give.
>
> And when He had prayed for the third time all anxiety and dread were gone. He had no longer any wish of His own. With words in which He sought to impart to them some of the courage He had gained, He awakened His friends from their sleep, and went with calm spirit and holy firmness to meet the traitor.[26]

Though Schleiermacher denies that prayer can influence God, it is not to be neglected; neither is action. Neither action nor prayer is sufficient for the Christian life. Right prayer only arises when we are engaged in the activities that go to fulfill our Christian vocation.[27] Every true prayer rests on an element of action. Prayer and action are indissolubly tied together for Schleiermacher.

LUDWIG FEUERBACH

Kant and Schleiermacher interpreted prayer as the human means of cultivating the disposition to moral obedience or the bringing of one's whole life into positive relationship with the Kingdom of God and held that prayer, while it might change the one who prayed, could not change or influence God's action. Ludwig Feuerbach (1804–1872) carried this theme further. Prayer could not influence God or God's action—not because of the nature of God, but because what religious people called God is simply a projection of their own humanity. There is no God, he declared, in the sense of a being metaphysically independent of and in one or another way superior to man. This view does not render either religion or prayer meaningless or unimportant. It simply points to what their real meaning is.

Since Feuerbach's rich and interesting view of prayer depends on his conceptions of "God" and man, let us examine these notions. The Old Testament God, Jehovah, is for Feuerbach the objectification of the self-consciousness of Israel as the absolute being. Jehovah is the personification of a national existence—or a political community—for which religion takes the form of Law. The Christian's "God" is the personification of his own subjective human nature, freed from the limits of nationality. The highest idea, the God of unpolitical, unworldly feeling, is love. For the Christian,

God is the Love that satisfies our wishes, our emotional wants; he is himself the realized wish of the heart, the wish exalted to the certainty of its fulfillment, of its reality, to that undoubting certainty before which no contradiction of the understanding, no difficulty of experience or of the external world maintains its ground.

Or again: "God is the nature of human feeling, unlimited pure feeling, made objective. . . . When one prays —the God who hears the prayer is the 'echo' of our cry of anguish."[28]

According to Feuerbach, man must give utterance to his pain, but nature is callous to his sorrows, so he turns within. There he finds an audience for his griefs. God is this "open ear of the heart." "God is a tear of love, shed in the deepest concealment over human misery." Quoting the mystic Sebastian Frank, Feuerbach writes:

"God is an unutterable sigh, lying in the depths of the heart."[29]

For Feuerbach, as for Schleiermacher, prayer reveals the ultimate essence of religion—not all prayer, but "the prayer pregnant with sorrow, the prayer of disconsolate love, the prayer that expresses the power of the heart that crushes man to the ground, the prayer which begins in despair and ends in rapture."[30] This is so because it is in prayer that man most elementally carries through the religious reality. He objectifies that which is a part of himself and addresses it as Thou. In so doing he affirms his confidence in the heart's own nature over against the structures of natural causation. "Prayer is the absolute relation of the human heart to itself, to its own nature; . . . a dialogue of man with himself, with his heart."[31]

Prayer is virtually, even when it is not actually, speech. Its effectiveness depends on its being intelligibly expressed, for in this way man "makes his heart objective," and this objectification makes possible the moral power of prayer. Prayer not only requires concentration, it is itself concentration, the dismissal of what distracts or disturbs. For this reason, too, social prayer is more effectual than isolated prayer, for in community emotion is enhanced and confidence heightened.

Prayer may express a sense of dependence, according to Feuerbach, but more than dependence is involved. The "more" is trusting that its concerns are objects of the Absolute Being. The relation of trust transcends mere dependence as does the relation of a child to a father. It is a relation of love, Feuerbach declares, calling attention to the fact that the most intimate form of address in prayer is the word "Father."

Thus in prayer one turns to the Omnipotence of Goodness, "which for the sake of the salvation of man makes the impossible possible." Faith in this omnipotence is really faith "in the unreality of the external world, of objectivity—faith in the absolute reality of man's emotional nature."[32] When man turns to the omnipotence of God, what he is really doing is absolutizing his own inner feelings.

ALBRECHT RITSCHL

The theology of Albrecht Ritschl (1822–1889) and his followers provided the immediate context out of which the newer theologies of the twentieth century developed. It was against the Ritschlian theology that the new theology rebelled. The heart of Ritschl's theology is the claim that man's reconciliation with God makes possible a new style of life grounded in that changed relationship with God. Where there had been sin or fundamental mistrust, now for those in the Christian community there is trust in the divine providence. Trust in the providence of God means being able to live in the confidence that "all evil as well as good is ordered for our development."[33] The ministry of Jesus has made this trust possible and has thereby made a new life-style possible for members of his community. This new lifestyle Ritschl calls "lordship over the world," a lordship that involves the sense of being freed from subservience to the world and from fear before "death, life, angels, and principalities."[34] The Christian life is delivered from destructive anxiety and is marked by what Ritschl calls religious and ethical virtues. The religious virtues are humility, patience, and prayer. *Humility* is man's willing submission to God. In this sense humility is the whole of religion. *Patience* is humility's correlative. It characterizes the life of those who see the evils of life against the background of divine providence. It enables man to maintain his stability in the face of either evil or good fortune. *Prayer* is man's thankful response to God's reconciliation and his providential care.

"Prayer is represented . . . as a whole and under all circumstances as thanksgiving, acclamation, praise, recognition, and worship of God."[35] Prayer is thus directly related to faith, to trust in God's providence and God's forgiveness. It is an expression of faith and of humility, for the gratitude expressed by prayer exemplifies the willing submission, no matter what, to God and God's beneficent will. What is otherwise present in man as "an obscure idea or as a tone of feeling" prayer brings to clear representation.[36] According to Ritschl there are two motives for prayer, which tries to bring clear representation to what might otherwise be obscure or inarticulate feeling. The first is to allow these religious functions to be shared "in common and in accord." This is what prayer can do for the church as Christian community. The second is to help "the individual . . . insure his faith in providence and his humility against those hindrances which arise, partly from contact with the secular world, partly from causes which lead him to doubt the security of his own religious convictions."[37] Prayer, then, is the way in which the community and the individual clarify, articulate, and reinforce their basic response to God in the face of unclarity, doubt, and whatever might hinder that response. "Prayer is the expression of humility and patience and the means of confirming oneself in these virtues."[38]

Ritschl says that prayer (or its equivalent in all religions) is originally the "product and proof of man's resolve to recognize his subjection to God in whatever character He may be believed in."[39] Since Christians believe in a God understood as love, as providence, as one who has reconciled through forgiveness, prayer will always be an expression of thanksgiving and joy. Even if prayer takes a petitionary form, we will "only ask something when thanking Him at the same time."[40] And since there is a danger that we might pray for something which in God's will we should not receive, the fact that prayer is also an expression of and a means of confirming one's humility, and that humility is the willing submission to God, guarantees that prayer is kept within its boundaries.

Ritschl develops his view of the priority of thanksgiving over petition by considering Jesus' own teaching in the Lord's Prayer. He thinks Jesus emphasizes thanksgiving as he himself does. He criticizes Schleiermacher's description of prayer as related to the future, to human anticipation and wishing, and hence to petition, as being unbiblical and pietistic, and he finds in Paul confirmation for his own views. For "the Christian Church thanksgiving as an acknowledgment of God stands higher than petition."[41] Thanksgiving is not simply one species of prayer alongside petition. Rather, it is "the general form of prayer, while petition is merely a modification of thanksgiving to God."[42] It is the Christian's assurance of reconciliation which more narrowly limits petition than does for example the Old Testament. The Christian will not, like the psalmist, call upon God to vindicate his rights or slay his foes so that he can then thank God. God's reconciliation and guiding providence are already the ground for thanksgiving, no matter what happens or what we hope for.

More than this, in consequence of reconciliation Christians rejoice always, even in distress and persecution. Otherwise, Paul's injunction is unintelligible.

But in joy we have no wishes, no intense desire for anything not attained; or if wishes do arise, we have them in joy without the pain which springs from their delayed fulfillment. Thus we are in a position to present them to God with thanksgiving, with an acknowledgment, reassuring to ourselves, of His power and goodness.[43]

If that attitude is sometimes not present, then, says Ritschl, prayer can be the means of bringing it forth.

WILHELM HERRMANN

Barth has called Wilhelm Herrmann (1846–1922) Ritschl's most reliable disciple. An examination of Herr-

mann's view of prayer confirms Barth's assessment.
Herrmann is almost an echo of Ritschl in his interpretation of prayer, though his rhetoric seems to disclose a
warmer personal piety and he leans heavily on Luther
for confirmation of his views.

For Herrmann, prayer is real communion with God.
It is "the expression of human need before God, the
expression of satisfied need in the prayer of thanksgiving, and of need still felt in the prayer of supplication."[44] Yet to define prayer in this fashion is not sufficient, for it does not make clear that prayer is the
response to God's initiative. Prayer is not the simple cry
of agony of a helpless man. A supplication "wrung from
the heart by trouble, and the idea, born of the wish of
the tortured soul, that an Almighty God will break the
chains of cause and effect—these are not the elements
which make Christian prayer."[45] Prayer is communion,
and communion is grounded in God's appearance to us
in Christ. The reality of God is not self-evident. We only
know the reality of God when we feel him "laying hold
of us when the appearance of Jesus becomes an experience of our own."[46] He is then known personally as
"that power of goodness which, with victorious love,
throws down all the barriers which divide us from what
is good. Hence Christian piety can only arise in the field
of man's moral experience."[47] Prayer begins in God's
revelation of himself. It is the result of God's creation
in the Christian of the desire to seek Him above all else.
For the Christian, even petitions that seem to be
grounded in particular human needs arise from this
overpowering desire to seek God.

Prayer is thus related directly to faith and faith to
prayer. In fact, according to Luther "a true faith is
nothing other than simple prayer." It is unceasing
prayer in the form of a continual turning of the heart
toward God, a turning that goes on steadily amid all our
work.[48] Special prayers arise from the confidence already existing "that a message from God has been re-

ceived and understood."[49] In its essence it is an "act of praise and thanks to the Almighty God, whose love has found its way to us before we have sought Him."[50]

Yet special prayers are not simply praise and thanksgiving. Each step in life is burdened with particular troubles. Jesus directed his followers to urgent and trustful prayer without reservation or limitation. This, says Herrmann, might be interpreted by some to mean that God "would grant every self-indulgent and selfish wish." This is not the case. A prayer that expresses only burning desire for some worldly concern is not a sincere prayer. It is only a seeming prayer, "for while the petitioner pretends to address God, his representation of God is only an amplification of his wish."[51] If the eye has been opened in faith, then any petition, Herrmann seems to believe, is more than a petition, for it is grounded in longing for God. Petitionary prayer is therefore legitimate, for we always are in need, and with respect to such need "faith can continue to be a reception from the infinite fullness of God as it was originally." In every position of life we can turn to prayer, asking "for the removal of its distress from the God of whose life and presence it is conscious."[52] When we receive comfort from God we are "turning to a Personal Power, with confidence that He will strengthen us beyond all our expectation, and will lead us through the present darkness into a marvellous light."[53] Prayer is an application of faith to the particular circumstances of the moment.

Such prayer is thanksgiving, even when it takes the form of supplication. It is the living unity between "the heartfelt desire to receive special help from God, and the humble (i.e., joyful) submission to God's will."[54] These two are united in faith, a faith which is assured, not that it can by importuning influence God, but that we are in faith before a God whose help is certain. Our natural desire to influence God vanishes in Christian prayer "because we feel that our supplications are laid before a God who loves us more than a father or mother can."[55]

Does this mean that we should not ask God for earthly blessings? No. Such a refinement of prayer would empty it of all meaning. We should bring before God whatever burdens the soul. When we do this, "then the confidence which he calls forth within us takes away the burden from our soul."[56] As Luther says, the one who prays finds he is helped: "God gives him power to bear his troubles and to overcome them, which is just the same thing as taking his troubles away from him."[57] Herrmann writes:

The natural desire that is born of the passion of the creature, and the joy in God and His will which He Himself awakens, must be blended together in a Christian prayer. But no advice, however careful, can direct us how to balance the two exactly in any individual instance. God alone solves the problem, by so touching us in His revelation to us that there comes upon us like a sunrise a wondrous pleasure and joy in life, out of which there is able to spring willing renunciation and patience under what we have to bear.[58]

In an article published in the *New Schaff-Herzog Encyclopedia of Religious Knowledge* in 1911, Herrmann addressed an issue that lay in the background of many of the nineteenth-century discussions of prayer. The basic question was whether, as the result of prayer, God would or could bring about something that would otherwise not have come to pass. This issue had earlier been raised in relation to the doctrine of God and the understanding of God's unchangeability. It could now, however, also be raised by Herrmann against the background of the new science and the understanding that nature itself was governed by unchangeable laws and that the order of nature, and of material cause and effect, could not be influenced by human desire expressed through prayer. Herrmann acknowledges "how difficult it has become for Christian faith to hold its own in the spiritual conditions produced by the progress of science."[59] Yet on the other hand he admits that faith is effective only "when it develops the confidence that communication with the God of the other world is a power over against that reality which is to be experienced."[60] The concept of a God who "opens to those who knock" is destroyed if it is considered that God cannot grant a prayer that will change a situation supposedly governed by natural laws. Herrmann argues that where a petition is merely the expression of human desires, such a conception of nature can only shake the petitioners' confidence, but that where it is rooted in the personal acquaintance with God and a longing for him, no conception of nature can undermine the petitioners' confidence. For the latter what we think of as cause and effect in nature is not the whole of reality, but only that part grasped by the senses. Therefore for the Christian "the thought becomes possible . . . that events in the world of sense may happen in virtue of his supplication, as God's answer to his prayer." The "limitless conditionality" of all empirical events, for the Christian, points "to the fact that God as the Almighty performs each of his miracles through the world which for him is a totality while to man it is a limitless entity." "Science," Herrmann declares, "can therefore not restrain from prayer."[61] While the prayer of power is never itself the desire to accomplish material changes, but a longing for God, yet if such longing is sincere, "supplications concerning earthly matters will always be interwoven with it."[62]

SØREN KIERKEGAARD

Creative theologians in the nineteenth century had, as we have seen, substantial difficulty with the problem of prayer. From Schleiermacher to Herrmann the theology of prayer was relatively neglected and the interpretations that were offered could hardly be said to make either prayer or the inner life of central importance. The outstanding exception to this generalization is the thought of Søren Kierkegaard (1813–1855). Though often regarded in our day as a philosopher or poet, and though having little influence in his own century, Kierkegaard has now been shown to be a religious thinker of the first order for whom prayer and the inner life were central to the Christian faith.[63] Had Kierkegaard been heard in the nineteenth century, the theology of prayer might have been different.

2
Karl Barth—
Neo-Orthodoxy

KARL BARTH (1886–1968) was a leading spokesman for the Protestant reaction against nineteenth-century liberalism called neo-orthodoxy or dialectical theology. Barth was first a pastor, then a professor of theology in Germany and finally in his homeland, Switzerland. His was one of the prophetic voices denouncing the idolatry of National Socialism. Barth was a prolific writer. His best-known works are his commentary *The Epistle to the Romans* and his multivolumed *Church Dogmatics.*

In his negative judgment on modern theology since Kant, Fernand Ménégoz called for a reversal of its anthropocentric starting point and its emphasis on human autonomy. Karl Barth's theology offered such a radical reversal. For one who was the child of liberal theology, trained by Wilhelm Herrmann, this change was as fundamental as those brought earlier by Kant and Schleiermacher. Barth offered a theology of prayer that not only put prayer at the center of the Christian life but that seemed to confirm its traditional meaning. No theologian in the twentieth century has written as much about prayer as Karl Barth and none has made it as decisive a theme either in theology or for the life of the Christian community as has Barth.

The centrality of prayer in Barth's thought is clearly related to his disillusionment with liberal theology. Symbolically, this disillusionment came to a personal focus at the beginning of the First World War as he faced the issues of a preaching and pastoral ministry in his Swiss parish church. At the beginning of the war ninety-three German intellectuals, including nearly all of Barth's theological teachers, issued a manifesto supporting the Kaiser's war policies. Barth wrote:

Disillusioned by their conduct, I perceived that I should not be able any longer to accept their ethics and dogmatics, their biblical exegesis, their interpretation of history; that at least for me the theology of the nineteenth century had no future.[1]

In his parish Barth found himself confronted by the "embarrassment" that is characteristic of all ministers —the embarrassment of the preaching task itself, facing the "expectancy that something great, crucial, even momentous is to happen" and then "to pray, to open the Bible, to preach, to sing—always of God, 'God is present. God is present.' "[2] To respond to this situation, Barth turned to the Bible, not to see what men have said or can say about God, but to see what God has to say to human beings. He discovered there "a strange new world," "the world of God"—not a world of human history, human ethics, human religion, but a world of God's action, of God's address, of God's word for us. He discovered that the "word of God is within the Bible," and this word is both the presupposition of and the ground for all that can be and must be said by the preacher, the theologian, the one who prays or sings. And this word which confronts us, and addresses us, and challenges us to faith or unbelief is none other than the Son, Jesus Christ.[3] Years later, when asked to comment (to a student seminar) on his basic method and intention in his *Church Dogmatics,* Barth is reported to have said: "If I understand what I am trying to do in the *Church Dogmatics,* it is to listen to what Scripture is saying and tell you what I hear."[4]

This new departure, which takes the Bible and the revelation it carries seriously, not only runs counter to

any anthropocentric starting point and dependence on
the supposed autonomy of human reason but also presupposes a God independent of all human subjectivity,
whether understood in terms of human feeling, willing,
or thinking. It presupposes a God who is an independent subject, one who is therefore absolutely an object,
one who transcends any human subject and who is
"wholly other." Yet the fact that this God takes the
initiative and reveals himself means that he can and
does interact with the human individual and the
human community. The emphasis on revelation and/or
a revealing God not only undercuts any approach to
God from the side of human experience, from feeling,
reasoning, moral action but it also corresponds to the
fact of human need and incapacity. The root and
ground of prayer for Barth is both the action of God and
the helplessness of man apart from God. If this is the
human situation, that man is approached by God and
that no approach is possible from the human side, then
the necessity of prayer becomes clear, for God's
approach contains within it the command to pray.
There is also the possibility that, not withstanding the
problem contemporary man has in understanding how
God can "answer" prayer, if God reveals himself not
only as one who commands prayer but as one who hears
and answers prayer, human prayer will be known to be
heard and answered. The nature, kind, and quality of
prayer together with the certainty that it will be answered and heard will be determined by the nature
and character of the revelation and of the revealer.

On such a ground Barth develops his theology of
prayer. Beginning with his famous commentary on Romans, again and again Barth returns to the meaning of
prayer for the Christian life and for theology. The norm
and source for what he writes about prayer is what he
finds in the biblical testimony supplemented by the
echo of that testimony in the Reformers. The critical
discussions of prayer in Barth's theology are to be found

in his *Church Dogmatics,* where he treats the doctrine of providence and ethics. Our analysis is based upon these passages, supplemented by material drawn from *Prayer: According to the Catechisms of the Reformation*[5] and from *Evangelical Theology.*

PRAYER AND PROVIDENCE

For Barth, prayer is the Christian's response to God's providential action. Prayer is what Christians do because of what God has done in Christ. God as Creator preserves, rules, and accompanies *all* creatures, but in contrast to all other creatures and other human beings, the Christian is aware of this providential action. The Christian perceives it, acknowledges it, wills to conform to it, and joins in confessing it. The three fundamental Christian responses to this providential action of God are faith, obedience, and prayer. For Barth all three of these responses are interrelated. Each is a form of the other. Together they distinguish Christian knowing from other knowing. They are not "law" but "freedom." God does not control human beings or treat them like puppets. He commands, but he respects human freedom. God acts and we act too at his command and invitation.

Faith is receiving the Word of God as Word of God. It is both a work of God and a work of man. It is participation in Jesus Christ and therefore in God's providence and universal Lordship. It involves belief, trust, and surrender. It also involves prayer. In fact, prayer is a primitive movement, the simple and basic form of faith. Faith moves from thanksgiving and praise, to confession, petition, and intercession, and then again to thanksgiving and praise.

Faith also means obedience—obedience in doing the Word of God, in cooperating with the divine work. Obedience is not a matter of law. It is a free response to the Spirit. Like faith it is a participation in Jesus

Christ, a cooperation in executing the Kingdom, and a free submission and discipline. As such it is also prayer, for prayer is the most intimate and effective form of Christian action, from which all other Christian action derives.[6]

But prayer is not simply faith and obedience, even as the Son is not the Spirit and neither Son nor Spirit is the Father. There is a "center" that distinguishes prayer from both faith and obedience. While prayer certainly is worship, praise, thanksgiving, confession, penitence —all these—what makes prayer prayer, what is for Barth its very center, is petition. Even where there is faith and obedience, one must ask how one is to live in faith and obedience. One must ask God to give the strength, courage, serenity, and prudence that are lacking. One must ask how to obey the law and accomplish his commandments, how to continue in believing and "believing yet more," and that he may renew our faith.[7] Prayer means going toward God, asking him to give us what we lack. Fundamentally it is asking, seeking. It is, says Barth, "the fact that [one] comes before God with his petition which makes him a praying man." The heart of prayer is the asking. Thus the model of prayer, the Lord's Prayer, is seen by Barth as clearly and simply "a string of petitions."[8]

How is such asking possible? It is possible because the Christian sees that God has drawn near, like a Father to his child. God has shown himself to be "Helper, Giver, and Deliverer." It is this surprising receiving which is faith and obedience and which makes possible the asking. We can ask because we have received this possibility of asking. And we can ask because we can know that God hears and answers. Prayer is thus a grace. It is grounded in the assurance that God answers. "He is not deaf, he listens; more than that, he acts. He does not act in the same way whether we pray or not. Prayer exerts an influence upon God's action, even upon his existence. This is what the word 'answer' means."[9]

The asking and the answering are grounded in what Jesus Christ is and does. In prayer, as Son of Man Jesus Christ is the human asking. As Son of God he is the divine gift and the divine answer. In himself the human being can do nothing, but in Christ as Representative and Substitute, the taking and receiving and the asking become possible. What this means is that because our knowledge of God is defined by Christ we know that God is with us, that he invites us to join his action. In prayer we enter into God's action because we participate in Christ.

Just as our relationship to Christ through prayer links our action to God's action, so that same relationship links us to our fellow Christians and to all humanity. Our prayer becomes his prayer and his prayer becomes our prayer, so that our individual prayers are both individual prayers and prayers offered in, by, and through his community, the church. This means that all individual prayer is also prayer in, by, and for the Christian community. Linked with Christ's prayer it transcends the individual. The "I" becomes "we," and "we" becomes "us." This is the significance of the "Our" in the "Our Father." Praying for himself, therefore, the Christian prays the prayer of the community. He prays "for the service and work of the community; and in so doing he prays for all men."[10] Thus, when Christians are brought together by Jesus Christ, "we are also in communion with those who do not yet pray, perhaps, but for whom Jesus Christ prays, since he prays for mankind as a whole."[11]Barth continues:

Mankind is the object of this intercession, and we ourselves enter into this communion with the whole of mankind. When Christians pray, they are, so to speak, the substitutes for all those who do not pray; and in this sense they are in communion with them in the same manner as Jesus Christ has entered into solidarity with man, the sinner, with a lost mankind.[12]

It is obvious then that Christian prayer is not simply self-hypnosis and self-manipulation. According to Barth, prayer is the very heart of the Christian life. It *is* the Christian's life. To be a Christian and to pray are the same thing.[13] Prayer not only is *directed to* God (one is not talking to oneself) but it *reaches* God. God hears. God answers. God allows prayer to affect and move him. "His sovereignty is so great that it embraces both the possibility, and, as it is exercised, the actuality, that the creature can actively be present and co-operate in His overruling."[14] Within prayer there is concealed the "finger and hand and sceptre of the God who rules the world." The individual "can expect and experience an answer in so far as he believes and obeys and prays as a member of this people, as one who is called to this service."[15]

PRAYER AND CHRISTIAN ETHICS

The theology of prayer is not only a part of Barth's doctrine of Providence; it is a part of Christian ethics. For Barth there is no independent ethics. Ethics is part of the doctrine of God. Ethics has to do with the command of God, with the conformation of human action to God's action. Christian prayer is human action. It is for that reason that Barth returns to many of the same themes relating to prayer in his treatment of Christian ethics. Ethics has to do with human action, but human action may be directed either toward one's fellow human beings and the human community or toward God. The Christian worships, confesses God, and prays because God commands such in relation to himself. These are direct, specific, and concrete responsibilities to the neighbor.

To make this point with utter clarity Barth again

returns to the theme that prayer is connected with faith and the confession of faith. In confessing our faith we acknowledge the receipt of God's grace. We cannot truly pray without at the same time "throwing in our lot with Him in confession." Nor can we give God honor without "again and again longing for Him and for what He alone can give—which is prayer."[16] But prayer is not itself confession, and clearly not the *outward* witness, though it leads to proclamation and though proclamation is grounded in prayer. Prayer is, rather, directed only to God. Prayer has no ulterior motive in relation to man. It is an inward movement toward God, even if it is vocal or communal prayer.

What counts in prayer is that one shall really be concerned with God and that one's whole intention shall be directed toward him. For Barth this means that the Christian can be free of care in prayer. In prayer we have not only "a permission but an order to deposit with God and entrust to him all our baggage (for one arrives with a very complicated collection of baggage when one has traveled through this world)." We can, says Barth, "entrust to God this baggage, which is at once temporal, material, secular, eternal, Christian, ecclesiastical, and theological."[17] In prayer there should be no other concern than God and his Kingdom. Any other preoccupation is infidelity, disloyalty, disobedience. We are to hand over our existence entirely to God.[18] Prayer is a kind of Sabbath rest from all one's cares.

That prayer should be "care-less" extends even to concern about how we pray. Prayer does not have to be beautiful, edifying, or theologically correct. It is, however, particular and concrete. Prayer is more than mere mood or feeling. It takes the form of speech, of inward speech, even if that speech is a sighing or stammering. One who prays has something to say to God, and he dares to say it. Luther was right, Barth says; "the position of a man at prayer requires utter humility as

well as an attitude of boldness and virility."[19] We dare
to pray because we have been invited, summoned, indeed, commanded. That is all that is required. However inarticulate we are, however miserable our words,
we can leave the matter confidently in God's hands.
One can and one need only speak as one is able. As Paul
says, we do not know and we do not have to know how
to pray.[20] The Spirit itself makes intercession. We have
the assurance that the "true and decisive Word which
can be heard . . . is heard already even though it cannot
be attained or uttered by man."[21] Yet prayer must be
from the heart. It is related to what Jonathan Edwards
called "religious affections." "If the heart is not in it, if
it is only a form which is carried out more or less cor-
rectly, what is it then? Nothing! All prayers offered
solely by the lips are not only useless, but they are
offensive to God."[22] If we pray with the whole heart, we
have the assurance that no matter how inadequate our
words, God will hear and understand.[23]

CRITERIA OF PRAYER

In the course of his discussion of prayer under the
rubric of Christian ethics, Barth undertakes the refutation of some of the challenges to prayer and praying
that had characterized nineteenth-century thought.
Prayer does not arise simply out of the fact of human
needs. It is not simply a call for divine help. Nor can we
understand prayer as useless because God already
knows our needs, or because God will give us his benefits whether we pray or not, or because God does not
and cannot change or be moved by human action. All
such challenges are false. Finally, the grounding of
prayer is in God's command, which, though it is an
invitation, a permission, a gift of freedom to pray, is also
command because it is God who invites, who permits,
who gives that freedom. Nothing more is needed. Nothing more makes prayer possible. As Luther, Calvin, and

the Heidelberg Catechism make clear, nothing can stand in the way of that obedience, for it is Jesus Christ through the Spirit who makes our prayer possible and who thereby makes our prayer necessary for us. Christian prayer has its origins in the fact that man belongs to Jesus Christ. If we understand this, there will be no place for pious or impious arguments against asking in prayer. What does it matter that it is the all-knowing and all-wise God himself who commands us to ask in prayer? What does it matter that human thought claims that God is unmoved or that human action can have no effect on God, when God himself declares that he hears and answers prayer? What does it matter if we can do nothing, if God can do all?

This is the first criterion of Christian prayer, that it arises out of the Christian's God-given freedom and that it is an obedient response to that gift and its possibility.

The second criterion of Christian prayer is that it is decisively petition. This is critical not only because the asking is commanded but also because it discloses the truth about God and the truth about man. It shows that God is the source of all good and that man is utterly dependent, in need of everything. It does not matter whether the individual has relationships with others or with a community. His individual and collective condition is, apart from God, utter helplessness and sinful creatureliness. Prayer has no external function or service. It is what it is, not a means of self-improvement, not a spiritual discipline like Ignatius Loyola's spiritual exercises, not an adjunct to psychotherapy, but quite simply the God-ordered expression of one's relationship to God.[24] That prayer includes thanksgiving and repentance Barth does not deny, but for him, in contrast with his nineteenth-century liberal predecessors, the thanksgiving and repentance are reflections of the fact that the man who asks is empty-handed and that he is a sinner and can only repent. One asks because one is thankful, one confesses one's sin because one is in the position of having to ask, since one must ask for forgiveness. Thanksgiving and confession of sin without the recognition of one's need to ask would for Barth not be prayer at all.

The third criterion of prayer is its "we" character. This "we" is ontological, not homiletical. It is either the we of whom I am one, or the I as one of the fellowship. All genuine prayer must have this "we" character, a "we" which includes not only all those of the Christian community but all mankind and the world. Barth underlines this theme again and again, and in Volume IV of the *Church Dogmatics* he adds a new note in discussing the order of the Christian community. He speaks of the relationship between the prayer of the individual and the prayer of the assembled community. Like individual prayer, communal prayer expresses human helplessness and creatureliness:

They cannot avert the sorrow and suffering of the world; . . . they cannot avoid their own misery; . . . they cannot alter the human situation. The decisive work . . . will consist in their surrender, . . . in the fact that they lay all things, both great and small, in the hands of God. They know that all that man can do can be helpful only in the renunciation of all self-help.[25]

Those in the Christian community must be united in prayer if they are to pray *with* "the One by whom they are united and who is Himself present in the midst." This One is "their predecessor in prayer."[26] The Lord's Prayer makes it clear that Jesus ranges himself alongside his disciples, that he takes them up with him into his own prayer. The community is constituted as community as it prays. Because its prayer is prayer in fellowship with him, it is never in vain.

For Barth the fourth criterion of Christian prayer is marked by this assurance that prayer in unity with Jesus Christ is never in vain. Christians pray with *certainty* that there is a correspondence between the asking and the hearing. The Reformers saw this confident hope as the *sine qua non* of prayer. Barth himself says: "The only questionable thing is whether our asking is indeed this wholly unquestioning action."[27] But Barth's assertion of the Christian's certainty that his or her prayers will be heard and answered raises the question of how Barth understands "hearing" and "answering." In his discussion of the Reformation doctrine of prayer Barth seems to ask this question in a very direct way. After indicating that Question 129 in the Heidelberg Catechism states that the answer to our prayer is more certain than our awareness of the things that we request, he asks the question, "How does God answer us?"[28] He then goes on to give what can only be called a mixed, if not an ambiguous, response. On the one hand he declares that God alters his intentions and "follows the bent of man's prayers." This is not a sign of God's weakness but of his greatness. "If God himself wishes to enter into fellowship with man and be close to him as a father is to his child, he does not thereby weaken his might. God cannot be greater than he is in Jesus Christ."[29] On the other hand he indicates that in becoming man the Son of God has taken our side and become "our Brother." "God has already made Himself the Guarantor that our requests will be heard. Indeed, He has already heard them." What lies behind this answer is Barth's understanding of the significance of Jesus Christ for the human situation before God. Jesus Christ is both man and God. As man, he represents the human, the one who prays out of emptiness. As God, he is the answer God has given to that emptiness and need. The work of God in Jesus Christ has already been accomplished. Humanity is saved. The answer to all human prayers has been given. Therefore we can pray, if we bind our prayers to Christ, that our prayer too has been answered. What we sought has been given. We have sought God, and God has given himself to us in Jesus Christ. This is our faith, and it is this faith which

carries with it the certainty that our prayers are heard
and answered, indeed that they have been heard and
answered even before we uttered them. That God
hears our prayers and answers them, that he responds,
means that we must do away with that "miserable an-
thropomorphism" and "hallucination" of divine immu-
tability. On the other hand:

God is certainly immutable. But He is immutable as the living God and in the mercy in which He espouses the cause of
the creature. In distinction from the immovability of a supreme idol, His majesty . . . consists in the fact that He can
give to the requests of this creature a place in His will.[30]

And so Barth can say that God not only *occasionally*
hears the prayers of his own, he *always* hears these
prayers.

THE CONTENT OF PRAYER

What then should be the content of Christian prayer?
If we are to take the openness of God to human prayer
with seriousness, there is a sense in which there is no
limit to the content of prayer for Barth. Nothing is
foreclosed. "The whole of human egoism, the whole of
human anxiety, cupidity, desire and passion, or at least
the whole of human short-sightedness, unreasonable-
ness and stupidity, might flow into prayer." One might,
like a certain American general, pray for the rain to
cease, says Barth. God is not uneasy in this regard, and
we need not be. The reason for this is that no human
request *can* be adequate. Every human request must
and will be sanctified. God rectifies every human request "by the pure hands with which [He] receives
it."[31]

Nevertheless, the Lord's Prayer is a model for the
content of our prayer. In the first three petitions of the
Lord's Prayer we will what God wills. We ask that we
may participate in what he wills by praying that his

name be hallowed, his will done, his Kingdom come. When we pray in this way, "we place ourselves at God's side, nothing less than that."[32] We do this because God invites us to join his designs and his action. In these petitions our prayer shows the universal character of the particular requests we make as individuals and as a Christian community. The last three petitions are a consequence of the first three. They partake of the same universal character since they follow the more inclusive petitions. They invert the prayer of the first three, however. We have prayed that we might participate in God's cause. Now we pray that God might participate in our cause, that he might respond to the basic needs shared by human beings. We disclose our dependence and we acknowledge that we cannot "live without God." We cannot eat or drink, love or hate, justify ourselves or save ourselves, be sad or gay, hope or despair, succeed or fail without God. We are creatures. But that we are creatures means not only that we are not without God, but also that we are nothing without him. The conjunction of the last three petitions with the first three means that what we need and want must be made to fit into God's design and God's action. The human and the divine are linked together; "we pray for the two as a whole." This is the case because it is Jesus Christ who invites us to pray with him, and in him these two causes are one.[33]

Barth then goes on to explain the meaning of each of the petitions of the Lord's Prayer. "Hallowed be thy name" is not just a plea for the future; it is an acknowledgment that God's name is already hallowed, that God has made himself known in and through his Son. The petition is that this hallowing may reach its end, that it may "not be in vain that thou hast spoken to us in thy Son."[34] The petition "Thy Kingdom come" recognizes that the end and purpose of the world is the coming of the Kingdom and that the coming of the Kingdom is independent of our powers. Yet one who prays thus must already know this Kingdom, this newness, this reconciliation. So the Kingdom is both present and to come. It is already fulfilled in him, and yet we live looking forward. The petition is that our past may become our future; "the Lord, who has come, must come again."[35] In the prayer "Thy will be done" we pray that what has already been "done" in heaven might now be unfolded in time, that it might be realized in our world and our lives, that we might be liberated from the endless imperfection of our obedience. In all of these first petitions we pray, says Barth, "that he may let us reign with him. No less than that."[36]

The second set of petitions is concerned with us and our needs. The "us" is the brotherhood of those who are with Jesus Christ, but that brotherhood is open to the world, to all those who have not yet heard the invitation. Petitions of this kind are possible because we have identified ourselves with God's cause. When we pray for daily bread we are praying for all that we need for existence. It is because we are enlisted in God's cause that "we dare ask him to save us from hunger and death." "Bread" also stands for spiritual food, for the food that nourishes once and for all. To pray for bread is to pray not only for that which is necessary for life but for that which is a sign, a pledge for the wholeness of our life. Such prayer, says Barth, presupposes that we already know God as giver. What we are really doing in this prayer for bread is acknowledging our total dependence on God and asking him to make our cause his own.

When we pray for forgiveness we again acknowledge our condition before God. We are, says Barth, "insolvent." When we couple this acknowledgment with the phrase "as we also forgive," it is not implied that there is a condition which we should set for ourselves in order to get God's forgiveness. This supposed "condition" really is what is necessary for us to *understand* God's pardon. Once we recognize our need for divine forgiveness we cannot do otherwise than to forgive our fellows. Where the pardon of God is received, it becomes possible for us to forgive too. And yet even as we pray for forgiveness, or pray for bread, we know that God has already granted our petition. If it were not so, we could not ask.

The prayer for deliverance from temptation and from the Evil One is not a plea for deliverance from relative evil. Its concern is with sin and death, with what the Scriptures call the devil, with what Barth represents as the threat of nothingness which stands outside God's positive will. But even as we pray such a prayer, we know already that God has answered our prayer, that we have been snatched from Nothingness, that the very praying itself acknowledges not only the danger but God's deliverance.

If the Lord's Prayer provides a model and a guide for the content of Christian praying, the question remains as to whether there is any guidance for the form. For Barth questions about the form of prayer are not critical in the way in which the questions of content are. Prayer will be speech, though not necessarily vocal. It will have an order, though not necessarily rules. Since prayer is "before God" and not before men, theological or rhetorical formalities are not important. Though prayer should have a definite time and place, it cannot be programmed. It should take place in freedom and spontaneity. Whether a prayer should be free or formal is not to be determined by rule or custom. The decisive thing is that the prayer express the requests of a modern congregation. Perhaps the minister should make extemporaneous prayer as much an object of serious preparation as the sermon—equally responsive to the congregation, the historical connection with the earlier church, and the need for a certain stability of form.

PRAYER AND THE THEOLOGIAN

A persistent theme in all Barth's theological work, one that is strikingly emphasized in his early works (e.g., in his book on Anselm) and then again at the end of his life (e.g., in *Evangelical Theology: An Introduction*), is that of the absolutely critical and indispensable relationship of prayer to the work of the theologian. The importance of Barth's work on Anselm can hardly be overemphasized. In the Preface to the second edition he writes: "In this book on Anselm I am working with a vital key, if not the key to understanding of that whole process of thought that has impressed me more and more in my *Church Dogmatics* as the only proper one to theology."[37] What Barth is pointing to is his understanding of what theology is and how it is to be carried on. Theology is faith's search for understanding, part of the act and response of faith. It must therefore be undertaken in prayer. Speaking of the faith, knowledge, and obedience which is the goal, Barth writes: "In the end the fact that it reaches its goal is grace, both with regard to the perception of the goal and the human effort to reach it; and therefore in the last analysis it is a question of prayer and answer to prayer."[38] This implies of course that the human reason acting on its own possesses no capacity for the understanding that faith seeks.

It was to this theme that Barth returned in one of the last chapters of his *Evangelical Theology*. "The first and basic act of theological work is prayer," he writes.[39] It is not that prayer comes first and then the theologian sets to work. Rather it is that, in its totality, theology can be performed only as an act of prayer. Theological work must have "the manner and meaning of prayer in all its dimensions, relationships, and movements."[40] Without prayer, theology is only human inquiry, human thought, human speech. But theology must begin and continue where prayer begins and continues, with the acknowledgment that "God is the one who rules," that man alone can do nothing, understand nothing, hear nothing. Thus theology must begin and continue in an attitude of prayer, by a turning to God, a listening to him and to his Word as a word of address. Human thought and speech cannot be *about* God. They must be addressed *to* God. "True and proper language concerning God will always be a response to God, which overtly or covertly, explicitly or implicitly, thinks and speaks of God exclusively in the second person. And this means that theological work must really and truly take place in the form of a liturgical act, as invocation of God, and as prayer."[41]

Since God is a living God, whose goodness is new every morning, who is free to "dispose at will over everything that men may already have known, produced, and achieved," theology must be ever ready to be renewed, "ever original, ever ready to be judged by God Himself and by God alone." It is in this sense too that theology is always an act of prayer, for the theologian must say: "Not as I will, but as thou willest."[42] And since theological work involves grace, God must be entreated for that grace. "Only when theological work begins with this entreaty can it be risked." It is the Holy Spirit that opens God to man and man for God. Theological work "lives by and in the petition for his coming."[43] Only in God's hearing of this petition is theology a successful and useful work. But God hears *genuine prayer.* And the criterion of the genuineness of *this* prayer is that it will be made in the certainty that it will be heard.[44] It is this certainty that underlies the courage to begin and to perform theological work, even the theology of prayer itself.

3

Henry Nelson Wieman—
Empirical Process Theology

HENRY NELSON WIEMAN (1884–1975) was one of the leaders of the "Chicago school" of American process theologians. His philosophical theology was influenced by Dewey as well as Whitehead, and by the social sciences as well as metaphysics. Wieman's work was most influential in the 1930's and 1940's, and through the teaching and writing of such students as Daniel Day Williams. A new interest in Wieman's ideas appears to be developing at the present time. His best-known work is *The Source of Human Good.*

Henry Nelson Wieman has been called by some the most distinctively American theologian of our century. Like Barth, he responded to the cultural and theological world of his time. He too sought to transcend the subjectivism of the then dominant theologies of religious and moral experience. His path was, however, radically different. Barth sought objectivity by negating human experiencing and turning to a transcendent Word known in and through the Bible. Wieman began with human experience but tried to transcend its subjectivity and relativism by utilizing an empirical method, broadly analogous to that of the sciences. He wished to establish the utter objectivity of God in such a way that God's reality could not be denied. His God, like Barth's, is transcendent. God is transcendent not only in the sense that he is beyond human control and, as Wieman used to say, "more than we can think" but also in the sense that he is utterly distinct from human ideals and values. God is the *source* of human meaning and values. Human meanings, ideals, values, are created. They come into being and perish. God for Wieman *is* the *creative process* that brings these meanings and values into being. Idolatry is committing oneself to one or another created value. Faith is the commitment to the creative good, to that which is most important for all human living. Prayer is one of the most significant ways in which the human individual and the human community can become open and responsive to that creative process which is God. Prayer becomes a means by which we make it possible for God to transform us and our relationships to others.

Like Barth, Wieman had a fundamental and enduring interest as a theologian in soteriology. In his intellectual autobiography he states his problem in the form of a question:

What operates in human life with such character and power that it will transform man as he cannot transform himself, saving him from evil and leading him to the best that human life can ever reach, provided that he meet the required conditions?[1]

Wieman struggled with this question throughout his career, trying to find ever more adequate ways of answering and trying to answer in terms that would be responsive to the currents of thought in the theology, philosophy, and social science of his day. Since Wieman's theology of prayer is related at every point to his continuing struggle to answer the soteriological question, it is important to trace the development of his thought through his major formulations. There are basic elements of continuity, but there are also important changes of both substance and language.

EXPERIENCE OF GOD

In his earliest published work, *Religious Experience and the Scientific Method,* Wieman writes: "Whatever else the word God may mean, it is a term used to designate that Something upon which human life is most dependent for its security, welfare and increasing abundance." God may be much more than this, but he certainly is this, by definition, says Wieman. If we are to know God, that is, if we are to know what we depend on for our being and our well-being, we will know God through our experience, for "the only objects we know are objects of experience."[2] Experience is not itself knowledge, in Wieman's view. We may and do experience God directly, but we do not *know* God directly. Immediate experience must be interpreted. It provides data that can lead to knowledge. When adequately interpreted, experience makes knowledge possible.

For the early Wieman there is a certain kind and quality of experience which is the direct experience of God, though not yet knowledge of God. He calls this religious experience. Religious experience occurs when the "bounds of awareness are greatly widened. The ordinary narrow and routinized selectiveness of attention is broken down, and instead of attending only to a few familiar data to the exclusion of all else, one becomes aware of a far larger portion of that totality of immediate experience which flows over one."[3] There is an "unselective aliveness of the total organism to the total event then ensuing."[4] The religious attitude is awakened when "the total object of all our experience becomes for us an object of contemplation."[5] Human life at its best is the search for that total Object in which all experience might be integrated and made to yield its maximum significance. This search finds its culmination in religion. Contemplation, as Wieman uses the term, is that kind of thinking which is midway between what he calls mysticism (sheer sense awareness of the richness of the flow of the totality that meets one) and the theoretical and practical knowing that grasps reality selectively by excluding whatever is not relevant to its instrumental purposes. Worship at its best is contemplation, a contemplation that is "finely balanced between thinking and mysticism," and that fulfills itself in action.[6]

Prayer is related to worship. In worship one seeks to open the doors to awareness. The Christian interprets what is experienced in this expanded awareness as making possible the transformation of the individual into the likeness of Jesus, and of the world into the likeness of the Kingdom of God. To the Christian, worship is a way of yielding to the will of God so that individual and communal life may be reshaped. Worship is giving the whole attention to God. Prayer is that movement within worship in which one focuses on enabling the transformation of the self. In prayer the persistent desires and past experiences of the individual become reorganized and unified by reason of the expanded range of experiencing that worship makes possible. This integration and transformation is the work of God. The awakening of the total personality which gives rise to these novel forces happens *to* us. Worship and prayer are what human beings can do, but the actual transformation and integration introduce a novelty that they cannot and do not control.

From this early and limited interpretation of the meaning of prayer Wieman went on to refine his basic understanding of God and of the way in which God is present and active in and through human existence. Changes in his basic conceptual framework brought changes in his interpretation of the nature and function of prayer.

ADJUSTMENT TO GOD

By the time of his second book, *The Wrestle of Religion with Truth,* Wieman was speaking of God in slightly different language. God is the "most subtle and intimate complexity of environmental nature which yields the greatest good when right adjustment is made. God may be much more than this, but at least he is this."[7] Wieman now uses the language of organism and environment. Life is the interaction between organism and environment. Like John Dewey he talks of the organism's adjustment to the environment in terms of habits, and he thinks of the self as the totality of habits, more or less well organized. To relate effectively to our environment we need a way of reorganizing that totality of habits which make up the personality. Worship is that way. In worship we seek to organize and adjust the totality of habits which make up the personality to "that feature of the environment upon which we are dependent for the best that life may ever attain."[8] "God" is the name for those activities (or that activity) in the environment which make possible the best that life can attain.

In seeking this best adjustment to God there are three stages. The first is *exposure* to God, "to that order of being which most vitally affects him, . . . exposing one's total capacity for response to the supreme demands of his whole environment."[9] This exposure Wieman relates to what has traditionally been called praise and adoration. The second stage is *diagnosis.* We must examine and diagnose what in our present adjustment is defeating us. Becoming aware of unattained possibilities, we see the destructive and self-defeating traits and tendencies we could not otherwise see. Wieman relates this process to what has traditionally been called confession of sin. The third stage is *reconstruction.* We try to establish new and more adequate habitual attitudes.

Prayer is understood by Wieman to be basically an attitude. It is an attitude of the total personality which adjusts the mass of habits called self to that order of the environment which is most beneficial to humankind, i.e., to God.[10] Worship is the way in which we try to bring about the reconstruction of habits and of that totality of habits we call the self or the personality. Prayer, whether or not it is expressed in the traditional verbal form, is a basic attitude that essentially "enables God to work upon us in such a way as to actualize the desired possibilities."[11] In Wieman's view, prayer is not talking to oneself. It is an adjustment to something that is both more than self and beyond the self. It "is prayer to an objective environmental God."[12]

GOD, THE ORDER OF POSSIBILITY FOR GOOD

By the time Wieman wrote *The Issues of Life* he was speaking of God as "that order of existence and possibility by virtue of which the greatest possible good is a true possibility and can be achieved by human effort."[13] There are many orders of existence and possibility and it is doubtful that they can all be reduced to one. The one order that sustains and mediates the possibilities of greatest value Wieman believes should be called God. This order is not static. It is a process. It is temporal; it exemplifies itself in time. Wieman is unwilling to call this God a person or a personality. Personality is an abstraction. It is not the highest value. What is of highest value is that which produces personality. The denial of personality to God does not mean that we "get no response from God." In fact, the response we get from God "far exceeds the value of any which any personality could make."[14]

Can one pray to a God who is not a person? Wieman asks. "If by prayer I mean the power of words to persuade God to do things, then prayer is futile and foolish," he answers. But if by prayer I mean the power of a certain attitude of the personality to so affect that order of interconnected physical conditions, biological organisms, and communicating personalities which yields the greatest values so that things happen for the good which would not otherwise occur, then prayer is efficacious and very important.[15]

Prayer consists in the deliberate outreach after that order of value which is God. Wieman then sounds a new note: the "order of God is like a fire that burns and a torrent that destroys."[16] The fuller entrance of that order into our existence means the destruction of our present way of life. There is a sense of either/or in Wieman at this point. Either human existence will relapse to the organic level of simple, unminded adaptation or there will be a fuller life of enriched communication. In either case the present order will be destroyed. "We can find our way to the higher order only through the flames of destruction and transformation."[17]

"Prayer at its best is the deliberate establishment of those attitudes of personality through which the order of God can possess the world. It produces objective and observable consequences."[18] Not only does Wieman suggest that the work of God will bring the destruction of old and present values and ways of life, but he goes on to suggest in his final chapter that the highest possibilities of value are unknown. They transcend anything that is presently known or hoped for. What Wieman's God may bring forth is beyond human ideals and imagination. In this God as the order of value and possibility there is the lure of novelty, of the unexpected, of the surprising. The most mature religious living, Wieman believes, is brought forth by the possibility of that which transcends our established ideals and convictions into the unknown and the unexplored.

Wieman explores other aspects of prayer in a kind of textbook written with his psychologist wife entitled *Normative Psychology of Religion*. The general approach is functionalist. Wieman tries to show the origin and continuing sources of human praying. But beyond describing the functions of prayer Wieman provides a philosophical justification and a normative interpretation and attempts to respond to typical questions about prayer raised in a secularized and skeptical culture. Wieman traces prayer to the impulsive cries of need and joy. Prayer has its roots in a spontaneous outreaching. It does not initially presuppose some invisible listener who can hear and respond. Prayer is distinguished from magic as it develops, in that magic is an attempt to exercise coercive power in order to achieve its results, while prayer is an attempt "to adjust the personality in such a way as to attain community of interest and creative interaction."[19] Prayer, as it develops, becomes a matter of customs and takes on many different forms, serves diverse interests, and is interpreted within varied religious contexts. Modern man, Wieman believes, is much perplexed by prayer. For Wieman the perplexity does not seem to center on the existential issue of unanswered prayer but in the erosion of the old intellectual framework by which prayer had been understood and justified. Many seem to think that the only reasonable justification of prayer lies in some kind of psychological explanation such as auto-suggestion or in a flight to irrationalism. If the basic problem is as Wieman thinks, it is all the more important to ask again, and in the context of contemporary understandings of the world and experience, "Does prayer connect us with a sustaining reality in a life-giving way, as breathing connects us with the air, as eating connects us with the life-giving power of food, as communicating connects us with those activities which develop and enrich human personality?"[20]

With this question Wieman turns to another favorite image, that of a bird which with outstretched and motionless wings keeps "adjusted" to the upper currents of air in such a way that it is lifted ever higher.

Prayer, says Wieman, is like that. "Prayer is adjusting the personality to God in such a way that God can work more potently for good than he otherwise could, as the outstretched wings of a bird enable the rising currents to carry it to higher levels."[21] The present confusion in our thought about prayer is the result of our confusion in our thought about God. Wieman tries once again therefore to restate the meaning of the notion of God:

God is the growth of meaning and value in the world. This growth consists of increase in those connections between activities which make the activities mutually sustaining, mutually enhancing, and mutually meaningful.[22]

Prayer is the attitude that opens the human to this growth of meaning and value which is God. Prayer is not then simply subjective. It reaches an objective reality that is superhuman, transcending the individual person and indeed humanity itself, a reality that does what man alone cannot do, a reality that transforms him even when his conscious intent works against it. "This reality of growth is superhuman because it carries man beyond himself. It takes man up, transforming his desires, ideas, ideals progressively."[23]

God, the Creative Good

Wieman was continually refining and reworking his conceptualization of God. In his most carefully constructed book, *The Source of Human Good,* he gives much more precision and specificity to his understanding of the process of the growth of meaning which he calls God. This process is now termed the "creative good" or the "creative event." It is contrasted with particular goods, which are termed "created goods" and is distinguished from all other values by being called the source of human good or values. When good increases, Wieman writes, a process of reorganization is going on, generating new meanings, integrating them with the old, endowing each event as it occurs with a wider range of reference molding the life of man into a more deeply unified totality of meaning. The wide diversities, varieties and contrasts of all the parts of a man's life are being progressively transformed into a more richly inclusive whole. The several parts of life are connected in mutual support, vivifying and enhancing one another in the creation of a more inclusive unity of events and possibilities.[24]

This process of reorganization Wieman calls the creative event. It is God, for this process is what brings all meaning and value into being.

Wieman goes on to specify the four sub-events that constitute the unitary process he calls the creative event or the creative good. The four sub-events are

emerging awareness of qualitative meaning derived from other persons through communication; integrating these new meanings with others previously acquired; expanding the richness of quality in the appreciable world by enlarging its meaning; deepening the community among those who participate in this total event of intercommunication.[25]

This nuclear concept of the creative process, developed in rich detail by Wieman in *The Source of Human Good*, is the basis for a fresh analysis by him spelling out what happens when we pray. Again prayer is set in the context of worship. Worship, for Wieman, includes the practice of ritual, which serves to loosen the coercive grip of fears and desires that obstruct the fourfold working of the creative good. Worship helps the worshiper to relinquish what stands in the way of transformation and to be willing to accept the hardship involved in creative transformation. The effectiveness of worship lies not in the words but in the influence it brings from previous experience, tradition, and the community's life together. "Prayer is worship plus petition."[26] Prayer serves to direct the sensitivity and responsiveness of the individual undergoing personal transformation.

What then is the "answer" to prayer? Prayer, says
Wieman, is answered when the individual, his appreciable world, and his community are changed in relation to what is sought in prayer. "The answer to prayer
is the re-creation of the one who prays, of his appreciable world, and of his association with others, so that the
prayerful request is fulfilled in the new creation."[27]

Petition gives focus and direction. If the petition runs
counter to the demands of creative transformation, it
will be modified by the transforming process itself. If
the openness to the creative process is maintained, or
to the extent that it is, each of the dimensions of the
transformation specified by Wieman as parts of the creative event will occur: new meanings will emerge; new
and old meanings will be integrated; the appreciable
world will be expanded; and the continuing and deepening of the community will take place.

From the human side then, prayer will involve sensitivity, responsiveness, and a focus of attention. These
conditions are required if the creative process is to
transform one's own person, one's relations to others
and the appreciable world. Wieman insists again and
again that words are not prayer. Prayer is a kind of
condition that should ground the reordering and
refocusing of "subconscious sensitivities" of the personality. Perhaps Wieman might agree that this is what
might be meant by "praying without ceasing."

Some readers may be puzzled by Wieman's use of the
term "God" for the creative good, since it seems on the
face of it to be a different kind of conception than traditional supernaturalistic theism or, for example, than
Barth's Trinitarian or Christocentric theism. Wieman
has many different reasons for using "God-language"
for talking about the creative good. In one sense his
views represent a kind of pre-Bultmannian demyth-
ologization. For him the term "God" has always been
meant to refer to the reality upon which human existence depends for its being and its well-being. The cre-

ative process, as understood by Wieman, is what does in fact create *human* being and what nurtures and sustains human well-being, i.e., human meaning and value. Whatever else God may have been thought to be, to be "God" has meant to be worthy of worship, to be of supreme value, to command an absolute commitment. Anything other than that which creates the human good is for Wieman not to be worshiped. No created good should receive man's ultimate commitment. Furthermore, whatever concepts of God human beings have had, whatever "gods" they have worshiped, if human good increased, it increased as the result of the process which Wieman calls Creativity. It was this creative process which was the effective agent that transformed personal and communal life toward newness and meaning. It is clear too that Wieman believes that the basic religious problem can best be met by commitment to the creative good. The religious problem is the question: what can transform man from the depths of evil and bring him to the greatest good which human life can attain? He writes: "The word 'God' is irrelevant to the religious problem *unless* the word is used to refer to *whatever in truth* operates to save man from evil and to the greater good no matter *how much this operating reality may differ from all traditional ideas about it.*"[28] The evil from which the creative process liberates us has four aspects: inner conflict, meaninglessness, guilt, and loneliness. Other expressions of evil, e.g., destructiveness of self and others, are derivative. It is the creative process which liberates us from these dimensions of evil. So too, for Wieman the creative process is related to what has traditionally been called sin and forgiveness of sin. Sin is basically unfaith, an inability or refusal to give one's complete and ultimate commitment to God. It is the creative process which in fact brings forth awareness of one's sin and which leads to confession and repentance. Operationally, forgiveness means that a change has taken place whereby "sin, while still continuing, no longer blocks the commitment of faith which is required for salvation."[29] Where there is a broken relationship between two persons which has been healed, the healing has taken place, sometimes even in spite of the intentions of one or both parties, through the creative process in which the four sub-events specified by Wieman have actually occurred.

Perhaps it would be easier to grasp the connection between the creative process and what traditional Christians have called God if one were to identify the creative process with love. Early in his career Wieman did identify the two. Later he wavered in making such an identification, declaring that the notion of love is itself confused and ambiguous because it includes much which is not a part of the creative process. Unless love "is identical with creativity and creative interchange," love is not enough.[30] For Wieman the creative good was disclosed in those decisive events centered in the life and activity of Jesus. "What happened in the group about Jesus was the lifting of this creative event to dominate their lives. What happened after the death of Jesus was the release of this creative power from the constraints and limitations previously confining it."[31] "The life-transforming creativity previously known only in fellowship with Jesus began again to work in the fellowship of the disciples. . . . It was the living God that works in time. . . . It was Christ the God, not Jesus the man."[32] When Christians see Christ as the power that saves, they are recognizing this creative process which freed Jesus' followers from the domination of created goods and created that newness of life and community, a life open to further transformation and continued growth of the good.

There is in Wieman's thought a basic continuity in his interpretation of prayer through his continued struggle to find more adequate ways of describing what does in fact redeem persons and their world of meanings.

Prayer is what human beings can do to develop an attitude of openness and sensitivity together with a focusing on goals for change so that God can work in and through their lives for transformation. Wieman does not try to go much further, for example, to spell out levels of prayer or to distinguish types of prayer. He does, however, go further than other philosophical theologians in developing direct and practical guidance for personal and communal prayer. In *Methods of Private Religious Living* and *Normative Psychology of Religion* he shares his views, based on his own experiments, of the basic steps involved in praying. The methods he describes were, he says, "helpful, sometimes to a startling degree."[33]

A METHOD FOR PRAYER

In *Methods of Private Religious Living,* Wieman describes ways in which human beings can intensify and deepen their living so that energy may be released in their lives and society may be reconstructed. These are ways of integrating the common and the trivial into purposeful unity, ways in which crises can be met and fellowship between human beings nurtured. The key to change is transformation by the creative process. His discussion is extended, but basic to all of it seems to be the method he reports in his initial chapter. A summary of this discussion will conclude our analysis of Wieman's interpretation of prayer.

There are certain preconditions if the process of prayer is to be effective, Wieman believes. We must be serious about the important matters of life. Seriousness is required if the individual is to venture out into the depths and be willing to struggle. We must be sincere about our belief. Sincerity here means being honest with oneself. We must not take into our prayer any beliefs which we doubt. "Worship is pre-eminently probing down beneath all the sham and pose, . . . getting down to reality" about oneself and one's world.[34] In such prayer or private worship one is trying to find out what is wrong with oneself and then to establish the personal attitude through which one can receive help from sources outside oneself that will correct that wrong. A third precondition is seclusion from distracting stimuli. Wieman thinks this is an important practical consideration because we are "to turn the mind away from lesser things and give [our] whole attention to the supreme thing."[35]

If we have met these preconditions, we are ready to begin. The first step is to "relax and become aware of that upon which we are dependent," sensing "that encompassing and sustaining and integrating reality" which, if one is psychologically able to use the word, one calls God.[36] The second step is "to call to mind the vast and unimaginable possibilities for good that are inherent in this integrating process called God." The third step is "to face the chief problem with which we are struggling, . . . surveying it as comprehensively and acutely as possible to find what most needs to be done." Next comes self-analysis. We must discover the personal readjustment needed and try to establish it. We must do what *is* in our power to provide the conditions under which the transforming power of God can do its work. Wieman uses two simple metaphors for illustrating this part of the process. We have to close the circuit, turning the switch which allows the electric current to be transmitted. We provide the conditions in the same way that we might bring together sunshine, moisture, seed, and soil so that the life-producing process can bring forth grain for the harvest. In prayer and worship we come into touch with the "current," with the life-producing process when we close the circuit by providing the appropriate conditions. A fifth step is to formulate "in words as clearly and as comprehensively as possible the readjustment of personality and behavior required," and to do so in positive, not negative terms.

Wieman thinks it important to repeat this statement again and again so that it can be embedded in us as a kind of "subconscious attitude."[37] On the basis of his own experience using such techniques Wieman reports "remarkable results of great benefit" to himself and to his associates.

Wieman believes that if we are open to the creative process, our understanding of our wants and indeed our wants themselves are changed as we pray. This openness to having our wants reshaped is, he thinks, the true meaning of the words, "not my will but thine be done." We must, says Wieman, think differently about prayer. "But our manner of praying, if we pray aright, will not be much different from the praying of all the great saints. They too were caught into a growth of meaning and value along with the causes and persons for whom they prayed—so can we."[38]

4
Paul Tillich—
Existential Ontology

PAUL TILLICH (1886–1965) was a German refugee theologian who taught at Union Theological Seminary, Harvard, and the University of Chicago during his American career. Tillich blended existentialist themes with ontological analysis in an attempt to interpret the meaning of the Christian faith both to believers and to contemporary "cultured despisers." His best-known works are *The Courage to Be* and *Systematic Theology.*

In Karl Barth and in Henry Nelson Wieman we have seen how the conception of God and of the human situation have been determinative for the theological understanding of prayer. We have seen too how their assessments of the critical situation in theology have forced them to rethink the fundamental approach to the problem of prayer in the modern world, the one by repudiating the pattern of thought of contemporary religious culture and returning to the world of the Bible, the other by pressing even further in the utilization of contemporary modes of thought to develop a broadly empirical philosophical theology that even more explicitly makes use of contemporary philosophical ideas and the concepts and methods of the social sciences.

Paul Tillich stands somewhere between these two efforts to interpret the meaning of the Christian faith for our time. Like Barth, Tillich finds in revelation the existential answers to the ultimate human questions, but the questions themselves are raised out of the contemporary cultural situation. Like Wieman, Tillich is fundamentally an apologetic theologian. The existential answers communicated in the symbols of revelation must be interpreted in ways that make sense to the contemporary mind. Some point of contact in universal human experiencing must be found. Tillich has no hesitation in using the languages of philosophy and psychology or in relating his thought to such formative interpreters of the modern world as Freud and Marx.

GOD AND OUR ULTIMATE CONCERN

For Tillich the question of God arises out of experiencing the shock of nonbeing. The universal human experience of anxiety reflects man's awareness that his being is threatened. The threat is both absolute and relative. Human self-affirmation is threatened absolutely by death, relatively by fate. Spiritual self-affirmation is threatened absolutely by meaninglessness, relatively by emptiness. Moral self-affirmation is threatened absolutely by condemnation, and relatively by guilt. The God question arises because, confronted by these threats to his being, man asks, in effect: Is there anything that can overcome this threat of nonbeing? Man's ultimate concern is defined by this question. God, for Tillich, is that which in fact answers man's ultimate concern, the concern which arises when he confronts the question of his own being or not-being.

In Tillich's philosophical theology the only reality which corresponds to that concern is God, understood as Being itself, the ground and source of the "beingness" of everything that has being, that which is the power and meaning of being, that which resists nonbeing. Theologically speaking, it is this reality, Being itself, which discloses itself through the religious symbols in revelation. Experience is the medium through which the disclosure takes place, but what is disclosed transcends the experience and the reality of the subject. For Christians the decisive disclosure of the reality which answers man's ultimate concern is through that symbol which Tillich calls "the picture of Jesus as the Christ." It is the picture of Jesus as the Christ, together with the New Being that it creates, which is the criterion of every other revelatory experience, although a disclosure of the power and meaning of being may occur in many other ways.

If God is Being itself, this means that God is not a being. It means that God is not a person, or a personal being. For many readers of Tillich this has created a problem. Tillich writes:

> The problem would not be so serious if it were not for the situation of prayer. The ego-thou relation is essential for it. Therefore God is not less than we. As the ground of everything personal, he is also personal in relation to a person. . . . But God also transcends the personal. . . . The reason is that God as Spirit means that he is not-personally present to not-personal life, personal to personal life, and supra-personal to all life.[1]

For many the question remains. Can we pray to Being itself? Tillich's answer is not exhausted by the quoted reference to God as Spirit. In ordinary speech and practice we think of prayer as communication with or address directed toward God. We address someone. We tell something to somebody. But, says Tillich, this is exactly what we cannot do. God is not a someone or a somebody. Prayer in its traditional sense is humanly impossible. This is why Paul writes in Romans 8 that "we do not know how to pray as we ought." What really happens in prayer according to Tillich (and, he thinks, also for Paul the apostle) is something quite different from an I-Thou encounter through speech. Prayer is paradoxical. "The Spirit himself intercedes for us with sighs too deep for words." The paradox is that "He who speaks through us is he who is spoken to." The paradox is "the identity and non-identity of him who prays and

Him who is prayed to: God as Spirit."[2] Another way of saying this is that in genuine prayer the subject-object scheme of talking to somebody is transcended even though the outward form of our prayer may have a subject-object character.

The transcendence of the subject-object scheme Tillich calls *ecstasy*. What Tillich calls ecstasy is the experiential side of a new unity which overcomes the independent existence of both subject and object. It is not a feeling or an emotional state. It is the form in which what concerns us unconditionally manifests itself—not simply in relation to the psyche but "to the whole person in his multidimensional unity."[3] The objective world in its richness and complexity (one's situation and one's relations to others) is not dissolved, ignored, or rendered subjective. Rather, the objective world is both preserved and increased. It is, however, no longer seen within the subject-object scheme or held within the dimension of self-awareness. It is drawn, Tillich says, into the influence of the Spiritual Presence and seen in the light of the divine direction of life's processes. Tillich usually speaks of ecstasy in connection with revelation. Revelation is this ecstasy, a transcending of the subject-object scheme in which what corresponds to ultimate concern manifests itself. But revelation is not the only locus of ecstasy. Prayer is its best and most universal example. Ecstasy is the essential nature of prayer.[4] Perhaps it is possible in this light to see what Tillich means by the paradoxicality of prayer. Even where prayer appears to be a speaking to God as an object for the one who prays, if the prayer is serious and successful, the subject is reversed. God becomes the subject at the same time that he is object. "We can only pray to the God who prays to himself through us."[5]

Prayer, and meditation as well, reunites the creature with its creative ground. Prayer and meditation are revelatory. "The divine Spirit grasps, shakes, and moves the human spirit."[6] Like revelation, prayer may be described as a mystery and as a miracle. It is the presence of the mystery of being. The veil of that which is hidden is removed, and our relation to it has become a part of experience. It is not a miracle in the sense of a break in the laws of nature, but it is miraculous in the sense that it is a sign-event in which the mystery becomes manifest. Prayer understood as "a conversation between two beings . . . is blasphemous and ridiculous. If, however, it is understood as the 'elevation of the heart,' namely, the center of the personality, to God, it is a revelatory event."[7]

PRAYER AND THE DIVINE SPIRIT

The paradoxicality of prayer has been related by Paul the apostle and by Tillich to the notion of Spirit. It is in connection with the symbol of divine Spirit and that of Spiritual Presence that Tillich places his view of prayer within the framework of worship. Worship is the basic response to Spiritual Presence, the "responding elevation of the church to the ultimate ground of its being."[8] Worship is the comprehensive notion; it includes adoration, prayer, and contemplation. For some, prayer might include adoration and contemplation, but Tillich distinguishes these from prayer. Adoration is praise and thanksgiving. It is *acknowledgment* of divine holiness. Prayer brings the *content of one's wishes and hopes* into the Spiritual Presence, adding something new to the situation which is taken into account "in the whole of God's directing creativity."[9] Prayer may therefore be said to be "heard" even if its manifest content should be subsequently contradicted. For this reason Tillich declares that Ritschl's attempt to limit prayer to thanksgiving is a mistake. Prayers of supplication and intercession do make a difference. They add something new. They change the relationship to self, others, and God.

Contemplation, which Tillich distinguishes from prayer and adoration, is the third element in the human response to God which is worship. Contemplation is the *silent* participation in that which transcends the subject-object scheme of ordinary experience. Tillich believes that every serious prayer includes an element of contemplation. He faults the traditional Protestant neglect of contemplation, attributing it to the personalistic interpretation of Spiritual Presence. Spirit, however, transcends personality, if personality is identified with consciousness and moral self-integration. "Spirit" is a symbolic way for speaking about God, or Being itself, in relation to the ambiguity of human existence. The symbol "Spirit" is grounded in man's experience of that which is the distinguishing human characteristic, that function of life "which characterizes man as man and which is actualized in morality, culture, and religion"[10] Spirit is that aspect of the multidimensional unity in which the power of being is united with the meaning of being. "Spirit can be defined as the actualization of power and meaning in unity." It is this experience of the actualization of power and meaning in unity which makes it possible to speak of God as Spirit and of the divine Spirit.[11]

Tillich speaks of Spiritual Presence in relation to the meaning-bearing power which grasps an individual or a community in ecstasy, breaking through the subject-object structure, releasing life from its ambiguity in a fragmentary and anticipatory way to a transcendence it could not achieve by its own power. This transcendent union appears "within the human spirit as the ecstatic movement which from one point of view is called 'faith,' from another, 'love.' "[12] "Faith is the state of being *grasped* by the transcendent unity of unambiguous life—it embodies love as the state of being *taken into* that transcendent unity."[13] Where the divine Spirit is present, where Spiritual Presence grasps an individual or a community, notions of "levels" or "degrees" of achievement or of progress are mistaken. The basic movement is from God to the human: "According to the Protestant principle, God's surrender is the beginning; it is an act of his freedom by which he overcomes the estrangement between Himself and man in the one, unconditional, and complete act of forgiving grace. All the degrees of appropriation of grace are secondary, as growth is secondary to birth." Therefore Tillich holds that contemplation in the Protestant sense "is not a degree but a quality, that is, a quality of a prayer which is aware that the prayer is directed to Him who creates the right prayer in us."[14]

PRAYER AND PROVIDENCE

For many, the most critical question that can be put to any theology of prayer is whether prayer makes any difference that reaches beyond the subjectivity of the one who prays, and if so, how that "difference" is to be understood. Does prayer make any difference to God, does it affect in any way God's relation to the world, does it change things in any way beyond its effect on the one who prays? Tillich gives his answer to these questions in the context of his discussion of the doctrine of Providence. When one speaks of the providential activity of God, Tillich says, one is speaking of one dimension of God's creativity. The notion of God as Creator, or as creative ground, is like the notion of Spirit, a symbol derived from the human experience of creative power at the human level. The word "creation" is "one of the great symbol-words describing the relation of God to the universe."[15] Tillich discusses God's creativity in relation to the three dimensions of time; past, present, and future. Providence is God's ongoing creativity directing all toward fulfillment and using all conditions toward that end. It is creativity directed toward the future. For Tillich, God does not interfere to change the constituting conditions or to manipulate human freedom. He writes: "God's directing creativity always creates through the freedom of man and through the spontaneity and structural wholeness of all creatures."[16] Rather, Providence works through the polar elements of being, through the particular conditions of individual and social existence, their responsiveness and their resistance, to direct everything toward fulfillment. It uses both freedom and destiny to accomplish its ends. To be more precise, Tillich says Providence is not an additional factor, some kind of outside or supernatural reality that enters into the ongoing reality. Rather, it is "a quality of every constellation of conditions" that "lures" or "drives" toward fulfillment. It is a quality of inner directedness present in every situation, a "divine condition" present in every group of finite conditions and in their totality.[17]

It is Tillich's interpretation of God's directing creativity which grounds the claim that prayer makes a difference and offers an understanding of how prayer can change "things." Tillich holds that a valid interpretation of prayer will not claim that God can or will be persuaded to interfere with existential conditions. Rather, it will presuppose that God is always active in and through such conditions. Prayers of supplication or intercession are to be understood as asking God to direct the given situation toward fulfillment. The prayers are themselves an element in the situation. They are part of the conditions of God's directing activity. It may be that the manifest content of a prayer will be rejected, but since the hidden content of a genuine prayer is the surrender of a fragment of existence to God, it is that element which is decisive, which is always "heard" and which is used by God's directing creativity. "Every serious prayer contains power," Tillich writes, "not because of the intensity of desire expressed in it, but because of the faith the person has in God's directing activity—a faith which transforms the existential situation."[18]

THE PRACTICE OF PRAYER

Tillich has little to say, so far as I know, about the practical aspects of prayer. He does not give instruction in how to pray, but at two important points he makes comments which are directly relevant to the practice of prayer. The first we might call his reflections on not being able to pray or on being inarticulate in prayer. In a sermon on the passage in Romans 8 which we have mentioned in relation to the paradox of prayer, Tillich speaks of those whose sense of weakness or whose doubt is so great that the experience of the Spirit and the capacity to prayer seem to be denied them. Just as for Tillich doubt contains some element of faith, so too in this sense of the absence of the Spirit, "the Spirit is working quietly in the depth of our soul."

In the moment when we feel separated from God, meaningless in our lives, and condemned to despair, we are not left alone. The Spirit, sighing and longing in us and with us, represents us. It manifests what we really are. In feeling this against feeling, in believing this against belief, in knowing this against knowledge, we, like Paul, possess all. Those outside that experience possess nothing.[19]

The second comment of Tillich's which is directly relevant to the practice of prayer has to do with language and symbols in prayer. Tillich's view of symbols is critically important for his theology. That God is Being itself Tillich takes to be a literal statement indicating what God in fact is. All other language about God is symbolic. Thus as we have indicated, God is not literally a person, even though much prayer seems to presuppose communication between two personal beings. Speaking of a God who is a person, or a Thou, or one who "hears" prayer are symbolic ways of pointing to the reality of God by analogy to our own experience. But symbols are not "mere" symbols. They are not "signs" which have an accidental relation to that which they point to. A living symbol not only points to but "participates" in the reality to which it points. Whatever else Tillich may mean by participation, I take it that he is speaking here of the power of the symbol to re-present, to communicate in an existential way the reality that it symbolizes. But it is also the case that symbols are limited. The symbol "person" is not fully adequate to re-present the reality that Tillich calls Being itself. This means that prayer should not be conceived exclusively in a personalistic framework. We have tried to make this clear in indicating that for Tillich, Spirit transcends personality. But Tillich would go further. Terms like "Lord" or "Father" may be problematic for some because of the psychological implications such terms suggest. Tillich recognizes the difficulty, but he points out that *all* symbols for the divine are "two-sided." They point to the transcendent reality they express, but they also are influenced by the situation of those who use them. Theology, he says, must be aware of both and try to interpret symbols so that a "creative correlation" between them can be established.[20]

Further, though Lord and Father are the central symbols for an I-Thou relation to God, an I-Thou symbolism cannot be the only one for our relation to God, for God is Being itself. This means that other nonpersonalistic symbols—"Almighty God," "Eternal God," and the contemplation of the mystery, infinity, and creativity of God—may all be forms of the language of prayer. In fact, prayer may move from one kind of symbol to the other, focusing attention first on one dimension of the reality of God and then on the other.

NON-CHRISTIAN MODES OF PRAYER

Because Spirit transcends personality, and because transcendent reality and the human relationship to it require nonpersonalistic as well as personalistic sym-

bols, it is possible for Tillich to give a positive interpretation to non-Christian modes of prayer and meditation. In fact, in his philosophy of religion, written in the
1920's, he interprets religion in a way that makes possible both the affirmation and the criticism of all religious
and cultic forms, including prayer. He wrote: "Religion
is directedness toward the unconditional."[21] This directedness is expressed through cultural forms. An object of meaning is sacred to the extent that it bears or
expresses the unconditional. The sacred or the Holy is
related to the cultural form as both "ground" and
"Abyss." The unconditional is affirmed through the relative, conditioned cultural form at the same time that
the relative and conditioned cultural form is itself ne-
gated. In breaking through the immediate form of the
existent, the Holy possesses ecstatic qualities. Here we
see a precursor of Tillich's view of religious symbols
which we have related to his interpretation of Christian
prayer. "Every holy reality *(Sein),*" writes Tillich, "is an
ecstatic reality, that is, one that bursts through its immediately given formations; it has an inner transcendence reaching beyond its formal, cultural given-
ness."[22]

All religion is this directedness toward the uncondi-
tioned. Religion can and does become false or inauthen-
tic when it loses the sense of the unconditional or when
it absolutizes particular forms, yet absolute or true religion is found in all religions. "True religion exists wherever the Unconditional is affirmed as the unconditional,
and religion [inauthentic] is abolished through its presence."[23]

Since the Unconditional is expressed in conditioned
forms, it is expressed in the sphere of practical action,
in "cultus." The aim is union with the Holy in dedication and appropriation. Sacrifice, prayer, mysticism are
all to be understood in this context. Against this background of Tillich's philosophy of religion it is possible to

see why he can give a positive interpretation of prayer in polytheistic religions. He writes:

In the moment of prayer the god to whom a man prays is the ultimate, the lord of heaven and earth. This is true in spite of the fact that in the next prayer another god assumes the same role. The possibility of experiencing this kind of exclusiveness expresses a feeling for the identity of the divine in spite of the multiplicity of gods and the differences between them.[24]

What counts is that in the concrete situation the God who is addressed receives all the characteristics of ultimacy.

Tillich sets the larger context for discussing his attitude toward non-Christian prayer and meditation when he deals with the issue of the relation of Christianity to other historical religions. He believes that historically the predominant response has been a dialectical union of acceptance and rejection rather than exclusive negation. A similar attitude is desirable in the contemporary world. "None of the various elements which constitute the meaning of the holy are ever completely lacking in any genuine experience of the holy and, therefore, in any religion."[25] That this is so does not mean that judgment and evaluation are to be abandoned. Indeed, the religious manifestation within Christianity must also be subjected to judgment and evaluation. By what criterion? The criterion for Tillich is Jesus as the Christ, the New Testament picture of Jesus as the Christ. This picture "shows no break in his relation to God and no claim for himself in his particularity." In the crucifixion the particular in Jesus was sacrificed for the sake of the universal. The image of Jesus as the Christ is no longer bound to Judaism, nor to the religious sphere. The principle of love in him is universal.[26] Tillich writes:

With this image, particular yet free from particularity, religious yet free from religion, the criteria are given under which Christianity must judge itself and, by judging itself, judge also the other religions and the quasi-religions.[27]

This symbol of Jesus as the Christ brings a judgment to bear on every effort in any religion to identify the unconditional with the conditioned, to turn the holy object into the Holy itself, or to deny the unconditional or the Holy by asserting that the conditioned or the finite has no ground or meaning beyond itself.

5

Dietrich Bonhoeffer—
Radical Theology of Worldly
Responsibility

DIETRICH BONHOEFFER (1906–1945) was a pastor, theologian, and martyred leader in the church struggle against Hitler. Bonhoeffer's sense of the worldly responsibilities of Christians and of the implications of a "world come of age" set loose new modes of theological thinking after the publication of his prison letters. Secular and political theologies of our day owe much to his seminal ideas. His central work is his unfinished *Ethics*.

Bonhoeffer's understanding of prayer is disclosed as much in his own life and in his practice of prayer as in what he wrote about prayer. Indeed, much of what he wrote about prayer was also meant to be a practical guide or was an outgrowth of his attempt to help students training for service in the Confessing Church learn to participate in a communal life appropriate to Christians. Some of it reflects as well his own struggle in facing the uncertainties of prison and death.

THE CHURCH AS SPIRITUAL COMMUNITY

For Bonhoeffer the meaning of prayer is firmly rooted in his understanding of Christ and the church. The Christian life is a life in the *sanctorum communio,* the communion of saints, the church, understood not as a human institution but as spiritual community. The church is actualized through the love of God, which in Christ's vicarious action restores communion between

God and man. Christ is God's will for community. Where human beings surrender to God's will in faith, the new being becomes a reality as human community, a living reality in love.

Human love is not of itself the energizing intention. It is God's underlying intention and will that energizes the new community. When the human commitment and intention in faith correspond to God's will, when in faith God's will is the ultimate and exclusive intention, then the church, the community of love, is realized. The church does not come into being through human beings seeking communion with their fellows, but through faith in God through Christ. It is faith that leads to the seeking of the other. The human communion that arises is a by-product. The less one seeks communion as such and the more one seeks God's will, the more the human communion comes into being.

The love that goes out to the other is agape. It knows no limits. It is the surrender of our own will to our neighbor. It sets the other in the self's place, loving him instead of ourselves.[1] Such agape does not aim at receiving love in return. It is "the surrender of the I, . . . an act of willing the Thou, but this very act proves and establishes the new I in accordance with God's will." When this happens, there arises a "new community of persons. Love finds communion without seeking it, or rather precisely because it does not seek it. Whoever loses his life will preserve it."[2] It appears that Bonhoeffer believes that if one deliberately seeks communion with others, something of the "I," or of self-seeking, remains. One would thereby be seeking one's own fulfillment, not that of the other alone. The Christian community comes into being only where we are fully for the other. Our being for one another is what the real church is.

What is the relationship of Bonhoeffer's view of the communion of saints to his understanding of prayer? Prayer is one of the three great possibilities for acting for one another that characterizes the communion of saints. The three possibilities, says Bonhoeffer, are: "renunciatory, active work for our neighbor, prayers of intercession, and lastly the mutual granting of forgiveness of sins in God's name." Each of these three intends vicarious action, abandoning oneself for one's neighbor, "to do and bear everything in his stead, indeed if need be, to sacrifice oneself for him."[3]

INTERCESSION: LIFEBLOOD OF THE CHURCH

There are many questions involved in Bonhoeffer's centering the understanding of prayer in the framework of his view of the church as the communion of saints. One of these has to do with the way in which he conceives the relationship between those who are praying for one another. For Bonhoeffer the relationship must be grounded in the notion of the spiritual unity of the church. The church has *one* life. The only communion an individual can know with God is through the church. Seen in this light, one's prayer is no longer one's own. It is the church's prayer. Bonhoeffer quotes Khomiakov: " 'No man is saved alone; he who is saved is saved in the church, as its member in unity with other members.' "[4] Those who believe, who love, who pray are in the church. "If you are a member of the church your prayer is necessary for all its members. . . . The blood of the church is the prayer of intercession one for another," writes Khomiakov.[5] For Bonhoeffer, intercessory prayer is not only the lifeblood of the church, but it shows what the church is. God's will is sovereign over prayer. If one doubts the value of intercession, one shows that he is still self-righteous, that he has not surrendered his own will completely to God. As an expression of God's will, intercessory prayer draws the other into relationship with that love which constitutes and gives life to the church.

But how, one may ask, does Bonhoeffer conceive of

intercession? When I pray in intercession for the other,
he writes, I move into the other's place. "I really enter
into the other man, into his guilt and his distress; I am
afflicted by his sins and his infirmity."[6] This is not to be
understood on the psychological level as a kind of empathy with those whom I happen to be able to respond
to. Rather, "being for the other" as expressed in intercessory prayer is grounded in our "recognition of
our own responsibility for the world" as guilty or, "what
is the same thing, of our own guilt in the death of
Christ."[7]

God willing, one can become a Christ for one's neighbor through such intercession. The guilt is borne by the
church, i.e., by Christ. By virtue of the church, one who
intercedes can "ransom his brother."[8] His strength
comes to him from the church. He is not alone in his
prayer of intercession. From God's standpoint, intercession is "the individual's organization of himself to
realize God's will for the other man, so that he may
serve the realisation of God's rule in the church."[9] Corporate prayer serves this purpose for the whole body.
It is the strongest means for organizing the whole
church toward God's purpose. Because this is so, Bonhoeffer thinks corporate prayer has a central place in
the Christian life. In intercession we

confirm the nature of Christian love as making us act "with,"
"for" and finally "in place of" our neighbor, thereby drawing
him deeper and deeper into the church. Thus when a man
is interceding for another in Jesus' name the whole church
is praying with him, but praying as "Christ existing as the
church."[10]

One might say that in Bonhoeffer's view the church
consists in such *action for one another,* whether the
form of action is intercessory prayer, renunciatory active work for the neighbor, or the mutual granting of
forgiveness in God's name. The community is constituted by the complete self-forgetfulness of love. It

rests in its entirety on the principle of vicarious action, i.e., on the love of God.

LIFE TOGETHER AND ITS BASIS

If one grasps Bonhoeffer's view of the church and the significance of intercessory prayer in constituting the *sanctorum communio,* then one can see clearly what Bonhoeffer was trying to do in his experimental seminary at Finkenwalde which he describes in his small book *Life Together.* Bonhoeffer had been serving a German-speaking congregation in London when he was called back to Germany to establish one of the new "preachers seminaries" for the Confessing Church. These seminaries were created in response to the severe crisis in the universities and in the territorial churches brought about by Nazi pressure. Bonhoeffer had given much thought to the kind of life and study that was needed to give adequate preparation to the ordinands in the face of the political and ecclesial situation. He had visited several Anglican monasteries and seminaries in England to acquaint himself with their training methods and their community life.[11] The seminary got under way with studies in homiletics, church and ministry, and the confessions. Most distinctively the group heard Bonhoeffer's lectures on discipleship, which became the basis for his famous book *The Cost of Discipleship.* But academic study was not all Bonhoeffer was interested in. In 1936 he wrote Karl Barth that he thought his students needed a completely different kind of training than that which they had received in their universities.

You can hardly imagine how empty, how completely burned out most of the brothers are when they come to the seminary. Empty not only as regards theological insights and still more as regards knowledge of the Bible, but also as regards their personal life.[12]

Bonhoeffer was convinced that "both theological work and real pastoral fellowship can only grow in a life which is governed by gathering round the Word morning and evening and by fixed times of prayer."[13] It was of vital importance, for a Christian setting to work, to learn what prayer is and to spend a good deal of time in that learning. The questions that he found were seriously put by the theologians in training were: "How do I learn to pray? How do I learn to read the Bible?" He wrote Barth, "If we cannot help them there we cannot help them at all."[14]

For these reasons Bonhoeffer instituted regular periods of silent individual meditation each morning on Scripture texts. There was group meditation once a week. Bonhoeffer himself took most seriously his own modeling of the practice of prayer in the community. He also introduced the practice of private confession, each ordinand choosing another with whom he could share the burden of conscience and receive absolution.

These innovations in the common life of the seminary led to a further development. Bonhoeffer proposed a House of Brethren, a community of some of those who had finished their study at the seminary, who would continue to share life together and who would be ready for new forms of service and for meeting emergency needs in the Confessing Church. This community would have a common life consisting of "a daily order of prayer, brotherly exhortation, free personal confession, common theological work and a very simple communal life."[15] The community was formed and lasted until the Gestapo shut the seminary two years later. Its dissolution led to the publication of *Life Together,* in which Bonhoeffer shared his understanding of the nature of Christian community and the part he believed prayer and meditation must play in it.

The view of Christian community expressed in *Life Together* developed both out of the theological concerns found in the earlier book *The Communion of*

Saints and out of the practical experience of life together in the House of Brethren. It also reflects Bonhoeffer's sense of the political situation in which he wrote. Christian community means community in and through Jesus Christ. We are brothers to each other by reason of what Christ does, freeing us from our own egos and opening the way to God and to each other. Christian community is to be distinguished from human community in which natural urges, powers, and capacities, as well as eros and common feeling for those like ourselves, are the grounds for relationship. Nor is Christian community a utopian ideal sought through eliminating the difficulties of relationship or through manipulating the processes of human interaction by psychological or social techniques.

Christian community is a community of the spirit, transcending and including unlikeness, the weak and the strong, those who will go on living with us through sin and need. Christian community is not based on some wishful idea of religious fellowship or some kind of peak experience, reached through spending a few days together. Christian community is grounded in faith, faith in what Christ has done and made possible. What Christ has made possible is just this kind of spiritual community which can continue in spite of difference, in spite of sin, in spite of triviality and weakness. Because Christian community has this character Bonhoeffer holds that "the most direct way to others is always through prayer to Christ" and that "love of others is wholly dependent upon the truth in Christ."[16]

There is in *Life Together* a sense of urgency that foreshadows Bonhoeffer's later life and experience. He declares that the privilege of living among other Christians is not to be taken for granted. The Christian does not belong in the seclusion of the cloister. "The Kingdom is to be in the midst of your enemies" (Luther), and that is where the Christian is to be.[17] Life together is a gracious anticipation of the "last things." "It is grace, nothing but grace, that we are allowed to live in community with Christian brethren." This fellowship may and can be taken from us any day. "The time that still separates us from utter loneliness may be brief indeed."[18]

COMMON LIFE UNDER THE WORD

The life of the Christian community is a common life under the Word. It begins the day in shared worship including Scripture-reading, song, and prayer. Bonhoeffer believes that the common devotion should begin with the Psalter. The Psalms have a special place in the life of the Christian, and Bonhoeffer's interpretation of their meaning is critically important for grasping his view of prayer. The uniqueness of the Psalter is that it is both God's Word and the prayer of men at the same time. How can this be? Bonhoeffer's answer also tells those who have difficulty using some of the psalms —e.g., the psalms of innocence or imprecation—in worship how that is possible. The secret of the Psalter, says Bonhoeffer, is that "Someone else is praying, not we." It is Christ praying in the Psalms through the mouth of his church. The Psalter was Jesus' prayerbook, and Jesus continues to pray through the Psalter in his congregation. This explains how the Psalms can be both God's Word and the prayers of men at one and the same time. When the individual or the congregation prays on the basis of the prayer of the man Jesus, they can be sure that "their prayer reaches the ears of God."[19] Christ is their intercessor. The church is the new humanity of Christ. Even if a verse or a psalm is not one's own prayer, it is the prayer of some other Christian and of Jesus Christ.

For Bonhoeffer, the Psalter is the "great school of prayer."[20] Through it we learn what prayer means, praying according to the Word of God and on the basis of its promises. We learn *what* we should pray for—for as true Man, Christ had the full range of experiences expressed in the Psalms. The imprecatory psalms and the psalms of innocence become possible because of his innocence and because of his taking upon himself God's vengeance in our stead. The misery and suffering expressed in the Psalms were also his. The Psalms also teach us to pray as a fellowship. In their antiphonal character they remind us that we never pray alone, that we pray with Jesus Christ. The repetitions in the Psalms suggest that prayer is more than a single voicing of human need, that it must be "an unbroken, constant learning, accepting, and impressing upon the mind of God's will in Jesus Christ."[21] Like Oetinger before him, Bonhoeffer thinks the Psalms are simply an expansion of the seven petitions of the Lord's Prayer. They show us that "in all our praying there remains only the prayer of Jesus Christ," which alone has the promise of fulfillment.[22]

Bonhoeffer returned to this theme of the importance of the Psalms for Christian prayer in the last work he was permitted to publish—*Psalms: The Prayer Book of the Bible* (1940). Here he makes it clear that Christians must *learn* to pray. We must not assume that the heart can pray by itself, that the wishes, hopes, sighs, laments, rejoicing are Christian prayer. Prayer does not mean just pouring one's heart out. We must learn to pray; we must turn to him who taught us to pray, using not "the false and confused speech of our hearts" but the "clear and pure speech which God has spoken to us in Jesus Christ."[23] And this speech of God's is the speech that meets us in the Scriptures. If we are to pray with confidence and gladness, we will use especially these words of the Scriptures, the Psalms and the Lord's Prayer. In praying the Psalms and the Lord's Prayer in Jesus' name, we pray them together with Jesus Christ, and in them "he accompanies us, and through [them] he brings us into the presence of God. Otherwise there are no true prayers, for only in and with Jesus Christ can we truly pray."[24]

After the psalm, the common morning worship should move to a reading of the Scriptures, proceeding through the whole of the Old and the New Testament, day by day. Consecutive reading of the biblical books, Bonhoeffer believes, sets us in the midst of the holy history of God on earth. "We become a part of what once took place for our salvation."[25] The reading of Scripture is to be followed by the singing of a hymn that is at once "the voice of the Church, praising, thanking, and praying."[26] Bonhoeffer favored unison singing. "It is not you that sings, it is the Church that is singing, and you, as a member of the Church, may share in its song."[27]

The morning worship continues in common prayer. We are to pray as a fellowship—common petitions, common thanks, common intercessions. Such prayer should be free, without fear, with full confidence, without criticism, no matter how halting the words. Bonhoeffer believed it would be best for the head of the family or some other person to voice the common prayer. Such a person he thought must be in touch with the cares and needs and joys of the group so that the prayer is not the prayer of an individual but that of the whole fellowship. Such prayer is only possible through the intercessions of all for the one who prays. "Everything," he writes, "depends on the fellowship's understanding and supporting and praying the brother's prayer with him as its prayer."[28] Though free, the prayer of the fellowship will be governed by God's Word and have a certain internal order grounded in the recurring needs and concerns of the community.

The spirit of prayer and the awareness of Christ's presence continues as the community moves to table fellowship and then out into the world of work. Prayer and work are two different things. Work takes man into the world of things, the "it" world, which helps liberate the human being from his own subjectivity. This can happen when one discovers the "Thou" which is God behind the "it" of the day's work. Bonhoeffer thinks this is what Paul meant by "praying without ceasing" (I Thess. 5:17). Christian prayer penetrates the world of work so that everything one does becomes a prayer, a "breaking through the hard 'it' to the gracious Thou."[29]

Where possible, the Christian fellowship should turn again to God in prayer at noon, but in any case it is united again in the evening at the table in devotion. "The prayer of the Psalms, a hymn, and common prayer close the day, as they opened it."[30] The evening prayer calls for special comment. It is a time for common intercession and for "forgiveness for every wrong done to God and our brothers . . . and for readiness gladly to forgive any wrong done to us."[31] It is dangerous for the Christian to come to the end of the day with an unreconciled heart. With reconciliation the fellowship is established anew. Finally, the evening prayer is that God may be with us even though we are unconscious of his presence as we sleep. This is the ancient church's prayer for preservation through the night.

This description of "the day with others" is patterned after what actually took place in the experimental seminary and in the House of Brethren. Bethge summarizes the practice of the seminarians:

The programme for the day began and ended with two long services. In the morning the service was followed by half an hour's meditation, an exercise that was not interrupted by the circumstances of the removal, though packing cases and youth hostel bunks were the only furniture. The services did not take place in church but round the ordinary dinner-table. They invariably began with a Psalm and a hymn specially chosen for the day. There followed a lesson from the Old Testament, a set verse from a hymn (sung daily for several weeks), a New Testament lesson, a period of extempore prayer and the recital of the Lord's Prayer. Each service concluded with another set verse from a hymn. Readings from the Psalms and the Scripture took the form of a *lectio continua,* for preference without any omissions. In structure this very much resembled Anglican evensong. Bonhoeffer believed that this sequence of readings and prayers was the most natural and suitable form of service for theologians. It was only on Saturdays that he also included a sermon, which was usually very direct. The ordinands discovered that he liked to choose hymns such as Tersteegen's *"Kommt, Kinder, lasst uns gehen,"* Michael Weisse's *"O ihr alle, die ihr euch im Herrn vereiniget,"* and Christian Friedrich Richter's evocative poem, *"Sie wandeln auf Erden und leben im Himmel."*

Bethge adds that the House of Brethren kept as closely as possible to the seminary's time schedule, but that at noon, during the time of singing instruction, the brethren would meet for a short period of discussion and prayer in Bonhoeffer's room.[32]

PRAYER AND SCRIPTURE MEDITATION

The Christian life is not simply a life together. It is also a life alone. Each dimension of life requires the other. There is an essential relationship of silence to the Word. The silence of the Christian is a waiting silence, a listening silence, a waiting for God's Word and a coming from God's Word with a blessing. The Christian needs the time alone for scriptural meditation, prayer, and intercession. In private meditation as prescribed for the Brethren, Bonhoeffer recommended attention to a brief biblical text. It is to be read and pondered for what it has to say to each as an individual. We expose ourselves to this text until it addresses us personally. We need not consider the whole text. We may want to focus on a word or a phrase. We need not be worried if in meditation things that seem to be extraneous— thoughts or persons—enter in. We can draw them into our meditation and prayer. If we have dry periods, or become impatient or self-reproachful, we should realize that we need only to center our attention on the

Word alone and leave the consequences to its action.

Scripture meditation leads into personal prayer. Bonhoeffer believed that the best method of prayer involved being guided by the Word of Scripture, for in his view "prayer means nothing else but the readiness and willingness to receive and appropriate the Word, and, what is more, to accept it in one's personal situation, particular tasks, decisions, sins, and temptations."[33] When we do this we may be certain of being heard, because it is a response to God's Word and promise.

Just as personal prayer must and can have a degree of particularity and individualization that corporate worship will not have, so too will our intercessions. Each of us will have those who are particularly in our care. "A Christian fellowship," writes Bonhoeffer, "lives and exists by the intercession of its members for one another, or it collapses. . . . There is no dislike, no personal tension, no estrangement that cannot be overcome by intercession as far as our side of it is concerned."[34] In intercession we bring the other into the presence of God, seeing him as a fellow human being and a fellow sinner who also needs grace. To make intercession is "to grant our brother the same right that we have received, namely, to stand before Christ and share in his mercy."[35]

Intercession is a daily service we owe God and our brother. It is very specific and concrete: it is concerned with definite persons, difficulties, petitions. Such intercession requires time and it should be a joy. We should set apart regular time for it. It is not a form of legalism, but of grace. For a pastor it is indispensable, and one's whole ministry will depend upon it. The test of one's personal life of meditation, prayer, and intercession is in the public world as is the test of true Christian community. Have they made the individual "free, strong, and mature" or "weak and dependent"? Have they helped to lodge the Word of God so securely in one's heart that "it holds and fortifies him, impelling

him to active love, to obedience, to good works"?[36] And
what one does in the day alone also affects the fellowship. "Blessed is he who is alone in the strength of the
fellowship and blessed is he who keeps the fellowship
in the strength of aloneness." Both are the strength of
the Word of God.[37]

Bonhoeffer's introduction of the disciplines of prayer
and meditation created a mixed reaction. At first there
were strange rumors in the churches about what was
going on at Finkenwalde. There was resistance within
the seminary to the practice of private meditation and
a special meeting was called to discuss the issue. Wolf-
Dieter Zimmermann recalls the initial reaction:

The spiritual order was what was new to us, a burden difficult
to bear, a discipline to which we did not like to submit. We
made jokes about it, mocked at this cult and behaved like
stubborn asses. Pietism and enthusiasm were for almost all of
us a form of Christianity which we rejected. Prayers in the
mornings and evenings, meditations, periods of silence—it
was too much. We were not accustomed to keep quiet if we
had words that could be spoken. Yet, apart from being a
salutary exercise, this "method" was a way of making the
common life of so many people bearable. Bonhoeffer later
told us that this second point of view had been very important for him.

He then goes on to describe what happened:

Each Saturday evening Bonhoeffer addressed us, as a pastor,
guiding us to live in brotherhood, and working out what had
been experienced during the last week, and what had gone
wrong. Thus we gradually grasped that this experiment in
life together was a serious matter. And gradually we became
ready to fall in with him and to do with zest what we were
asked to do. It did not come to very much, though. The time
of meditation still did not grow into a time of revelation; the
text did not speak to us, and if it did, it was in our own voice.
We complained to Bonhoeffer about this failure, and it was
decided to meditate together, and not in silence, once or
twice a week. With the help of what others found in the text,
we at least got an idea of what was meant by the word
meditation. All of us had been too much bent on exegesis and
application of the text. We had not known what it means that

the word preaches itself. Only through long times of waiting and quiet did we learn that the text "may be our master." Half an hour of concentration: it is amazing what comes into your head during that time. The mind moves around, memories arise, dreams awaken. Sudden anger flares up. When we told Bonhoeffer of this, he said that was all right; things have to come into the open; but they must also be tamed in and through prayer. Everything that is suddenly there must be worked out in prayer. For many of us that half hour remained a burden to the end. But it taught all of us that the biblical word is more than a "subject" which can be handled *ad libitum*. A text which had been meditated on can no longer be dissected into different sources and layers. The power of the word, just as it is transmitted, is only felt by him who bows before that word.[38]

A number of Bonhoeffer's students later recalled the way in which their training in prayer and meditation stood them in good stead in the difficult days that followed, and especially during imprisonment. One of the most striking things about the life together was the way in which through the seminary's circular letters the former students, and especially those undergoing particular trials, were bound together in a circle of intercession. The continued use of common biblical texts for meditation among those who were a part of the ongoing seminary and those who were its "alumni" bound each to the others in a circle of mutual care and support.

FAITH INCLUDES OBEDIENCE

Bonhoeffer had a vision of the meaning of Christian life in community and of the needs of the church in his time and place which informed all that he tried to do at the seminary. In 1935 he wrote to his brother Karl-Friedrich:

I think I am right in saying that I would only achieve true inward clarity and sincerity by really starting work on the Sermon on the Mount. Here alone lies the force that can blow all this stuff and nonsense sky-high. . . . The restoration of the Church must surely depend on a new kind of monasticism, having nothing in common with the old but an uncompromising adherence to the Sermon on the Mount in imitation of Christ. I believe the time has come to rally men together for this.[39]

It was the meaning of discipleship which formed the center of Bonhoeffer's concern in the seminary and in the House of Brethren. There was a discipleship of prayer and meditation as well as a discipleship of practical action and pastoral leadership. Faith includes obedience: "Only he who believes is obedient, and only he who is obedient believes."[40] One of the forms of faith's obedience is prayer. In *The Cost of Discipleship*, Bonhoeffer turns to the Sermon on the Mount to interpret Jesus' own teaching on prayer. We are to pray for "those which despitefully use you and persecute you." We are to pray for our enemies. This would be difficult at any time, but in the context of Bonhoeffer's time and place it must have seemed an impossible possibility. Bonhoeffer speaks of "the holy struggle which lies before us," of the coming widespread persecution, and he calls for prayer for the enemies. What will this mean? It will mean going in prayer to our enemy, "standing by his side," pleading for him to God. In the face of the cross we will see that, like the disciples, we too were Christ's enemies and that he overcame that hatred. "It is this that opens the disciple's eyes and enables him to see his enemy as a brother."[41] We too will pray that our enemies may have the same love and peace which we enjoy, "a prayer which will penetrate to the depths of their souls and rend their hearts more grievously than anything they can do to us."[42] The disciples learned that the only way to reach others is by praying to God. "He closes and He opens."[43]

In discussing the Lord's Prayer, Bonhoeffer sheds further light on his own understanding of prayer. Jesus teaches his followers to pray. This means that, though prayer may be an expression of universal human instinct, Christian prayer is not simply a natural activity. Christian prayer has a mediator. We pray because of Jesus, because he tells us we may and because we have faith in him. "This is what gives Christian prayer its boundless confidence and its joyous certainty."[44] Christian prayer is hidden. It is the opposite of self-display. We are not even to observe ourselves in our praying. The self must be surrendered entirely—to God. Then we can truly pray, "Thy will be done," and our prayer can really and truly be petition—if God is the sole object of our prayer. Jesus not only told his disciples *how* to pray; he told them *what* to pray. It is for God's name, God's Kingdom, God's will—and God's will includes man's daily bread, the forgiveness of man's guilt, for preservation against temptation, and deliverance from evil. These things are assured them by their fellowship with Jesus Christ in whom God's name is hallowed, his Kingdom comes, and his will is done.

PRAYER IN A WORLD COME OF AGE

For some students of Bonhoeffer there is a great leap from *The Cost of Discipleship* to *Letters and Papers from Prison.* Writing to Bethge from prison in July 1944, Bonhoeffer declared: "I thought I could acquire faith by trying to live a holy life, or something like it. I suppose I wrote *The Cost of Discipleship* as the end of that path. Today I can see the dangers in that book, though I still stand by what I wrote."[45] An apparently even more dramatic statement of a radical shift in thinking is expressed in his writing of a world come of age, of the ability of modern men to do without religion, and of having to live in a world without God— "Before God and with God we live without God . . . we must live as men who manage our lives without him."[46] Depending on their own views, some of his interpreters have—either happily or unhappily—claimed Bonhoeffer for Marxism, or for "death of God" theology, or for total secularity. And, more important for our concerns in this work, we find Bonhoeffer writing to Bethge at the end of April 1944: "What is the place of worship and prayer in a religionless situation?"[47] Bonhoeffer did not live to develop the full meaning of his new theological departure nor to answer in detail his own question about worship and prayer. Bethge has, however, given the best interpretation of what Bonhoeffer was struggling to express in his new venture and his apparently novel concepts. He has shown both the connections to the past and the novelty in Bonhoeffer's latest theological thought.

When Bonhoeffer wrote of "a world come of age," Bethge says, he was thinking of what Kant meant by "the Enlightenment," namely, a movement from immaturity—which is the incapacity to use one's own intelligence without being guided by another—to maturity. Maturity means autonomy, taking responsibility for oneself. As Bonhoeffer understands it, *religion* is a transitory historical phenomenon associated with human immaturity. It is grounded in a kind of metaphysical view of the world in which what is ultimate is in another realm. "Religion" is individualistic, trying to safeguard a place for God in inwardness, in the inner, private world of the self. Religion is a separate area distinct from the rest of life. God is understood in terms of "power," an "answer," or a "solution" or "medicine" for human problems. Religion is also used to rationalize and support privilege. It is used to perpetuate dependency.

For Bonhoeffer, Christian faith is not a religion in this sense at all, though Christians may make it into a religion. God is not to be interpreted metaphysically as a supernatural being. Transcendence is horizontal, social. The meaning of faith is not to be found in inwardness and in some private world. Dependence and privilege are not fostered by real faith. Thus, when Bonhoeffer calls for a "non-religious interpretation of

Biblical concepts," he is asking for an interpretation that replaces a false "religious" interpretation with one that can be meaningful to those who have no use for religion in the old sense. When he asks "who Christ really is, for us today," he is asking: "How can Christ become the Lord of the religionless? . . . How do we speak of God—without religion, i.e., without the temporally conditioned presuppositions of metaphysics, inwardness, and so on? How do we speak (or perhaps we cannot now even 'speak' as we used to) in a 'secular' way about 'God'?"[48]

Of course Bonhoeffer had moved in this direction in his earlier work. His understanding of the church's sociality opposed individualistic and privatistic versions of Christianity. His kenotic Christology of "the man for others," his horizontal conception of transcendence, his distinction between faith and religion, may all be seen as positively connected with the rethinking he was undertaking in the prison letters.

But what are the implications of these emerging views for his interpretation of prayer and meditation? Does the world's coming of age mean the end of prayer, or does it reduce prayer completely to moral self-cultivation as it did for Kant? Here Bonhoeffer's answer seems to be a clear negative. He speaks in the prison letters of the need for an "arcane discipline." The term "arcane discipline" is rooted in the early Christian practice of excluding the not yet fully initiated catechumens from the second part of the liturgy, in which the Lord's Supper was celebrated and the Nicene Creed sung. Even in the new day, there must be a secret discipline "whereby the *mysteries* of the Christian faith are protected against profanation."[49] In answer to his own query, "What is the place of worship and prayer in a religionless situation?" he suggests another: "Does the secret discipline, or alternatively the difference (which I have suggested to you before) between penultimate and ultimate, take on a new importance here?"[50] A

month later (May 1944) in writing a word concerning
the future at the time of the baptism of Bethge's son,
Bonhoeffer speaks of uttering the Word of God, saying,
"It will be a new language, perhaps quite non-religious,
but liberating and redeeming—as was Jesus' language."
Until then, he declares, "our being Christians today will
be limited to two things: prayer and righteous action
among men. All Christian thinking, speaking, and organizing must be born anew out of this prayer and
action."[51]

Though it is not clear from the fragments of the
prison letters what Bonhoeffer might have wanted to
say about prayer and the hidden discipline of Christians, it is clear that he did not intend to dissolve Christian faith into shallow secularity (cf. the letter of July 21,
1944) or to lose the identity of the Christian church. In
fact, Bethge points out, the "non-religious interpretation" means the identification of the Christian church
with the world. The arcane discipline is the guarantee
of the identity that can undertake such a relationship to
the world. "Arcane discipline without worldliness is a
ghetto, and worldliness without arcane discipline is no
more than the streets," says Bethge.[52]

More than anything Bonhoeffer says in the prison
letters, the continuing centrality of prayer is suggested
by the model of his own prayer discipline and his own
uninterpreted actions."[53] Readers of the letters cannot
help noting Bonhoeffer's references to his own life of
prayer, his intercessions for others, and his sense of
being strengthened by the prayers of others. There are
countless references to prayer in his earlier writings as
well. In good times and in bad, in crises such as deciding
to return to Germany from America, or in facing death,
Bonhoeffer turned to prayer. Perhaps the most con-
vincing argument that Bonhoeffer's new theological
ideas did not displace his convictions as to the meaning
of prayer is that he remained a man of prayer to the

end. The camp doctor at the Flossenbürg concentration camp where Bonhoeffer was executed wrote:

On the morning of that day between five and six o'clock the prisoners, among them Admiral Canaris, General Oster, General Thomas and *Reichgerichtsrat* Sack were taken from their cells, and the verdicts of the court martial read out to them. Through the half-open door in one room of the huts I saw Pastor Bonhoeffer, before taking off his prison garb, kneeling on the floor praying fervently to his God. I was most deeply moved by the way this lovable man prayed, so devout and so certain that God heard his prayer. At the place of execution, he again said a short prayer and then climbed the steps to the gallows, brave and composed. His death ensued after a few seconds. In the almost fifty years that I worked as a doctor, I have hardly ever seen a man die so entirely submissive to the will of God.[54]

6
C. S. Lewis—
Orthodox Apologetics

C. S. LEWIS (1898–1963), lay theologian and apologist for Christian orthodoxy, was professor of English literature at Oxford and Cambridge. His works of fantasy and science fiction, together with his popular expositions of Christian doctrine, have made his views known to a wide reading public. His best-known popular work is *The Screwtape Letters.*

Literary critic, professor of literature, writer of fantasy and children's stories, C. S. Lewis was and is the most popular lay theologian of this century. He was also a man of prayer who sought to share his understanding of prayer with his fellow believers in such a way as to meet the arguments of the cultured despisers of traditional Christianity and to respond to the difficulties that fellow Christians had in their efforts to carry on a life of prayer.

Lewis' views on prayer are to be found in a small book entitled *Letters to Malcolm: Chiefly on Prayer,* in three short articles, and in numerous letters written in answer to real queries from the religiously concerned. There are in addition some brief comments on prayer elsewhere in Lewis' writing, in his autobiography *(Surprised by Joy)* and in the profound and delightful *The Screwtape Letters.* The "letters" addressed to Malcolm contain further developments of ideas already present in his letters to real correspondents. The connections between the two kinds of letters show the roots of his interpretation in his own experience and in the real questions of others. Perhaps the main difference is that *Letters to Malcolm* is written with a dry humor unique in the literature on prayer. The presumed exchange of letters, of which the reader has only one side, allows Lewis to use his dialectical skill to introduce a variety of viewpoints. In part the form is straight exposition. In part it is a response to a presumed question or comment by Malcolm or another family member. In the course of twenty-two short letters, the three brief articles, and a few other passages Lewis touches on the major issues in a theology of prayer and offers practical wisdom on the life of prayer. Behind what is for the most part a venture into popular apologetic theology lies a view of the nature of prayer which is not elaborated but which is grounded in his understanding of the reality of God and of God's relation to the world. It is this understanding which leads him to define prayer as he does and to consider both the criticisms of prayer leveled by non-Christians and the difficulties in praying experienced by sincere Christian believers. We turn first to Lewis' grounding theological view and to his understanding of what he calls the "prayer situation."

Participating in God's Creation

God is to be understood as the omniscient, omnipotent, perfectly good Creator. As Creator, God acts more like a creative artist or musician than like the governor of a state or a "manager." The Creator does not act through "general laws" but in relation to each human soul, and perhaps each particle of matter. "If there is a Providence at all, everything is providential and every providence is a special providence."[1] In God's act of creation every being makes its contribution. In this act of creation, beings may contribute as members of the category of things or as members of the category of persons. Prayer for C. S. Lewis is one of the ways in which human beings participate in God's creation at the level of personal being. It is the way in which we maintain a relation to God which is personal and move toward a life of sanctity which is a union of our will and God's. This is both the human goal and God's goal for humanity. Ordinarily we are known to God at the level of impersonal being, but when we pray we are known in a different way. "The change is in us. The passive changes to the active. Instead of merely being known, we show, we tell, we offer ourselves to view."[2] From Lewis' point of view, this change is not a simple human possibility. It is the Holy Spirit which makes prayer possible and God's own will has determined this possibility. Prayer is thus both a means and an end. It is the means by which we are raised to the level of a personal relationship to God, for the world was made in part that there might be prayer, that God's creation might include this dimension. It is an end because it is part of God's creative plan: "The great work of art was made for the sake of all it does and is, down to the curve of every wave and the flight of every insect."[3]

Though Lewis agrees that for many believers it may be very easy to think of prayer simply as addressing God, it is not so easy for the intellectual to do so. Here Lewis is speaking out of of his own experience. "We have to work back to the simplicity a long way round."[4] The problem is that for the intellectual neither the "I" nor God are simple or clear ideas. The intellectual recognizes that both the "I" and God as they are conceived are "phantasmal." They are human constructs. They are, in fact, personal constructs. Somehow in prayer when we come into the presence of God we have to penetrate this "I" and the material context which surrounds us to that which "simply is" and that which is "sheerly real." Here in the momentary confrontation of subject and object is "the actual meeting of God's activity and man's."[5] For Lewis this is not a question of a God "up there" or "out there." The present operation of God "in here" is the ground of my own being, and God "in there" is the ground of the matter that surrounds men, "God embracing and uniting both in the daily miracle of finite consciousness."[6]

For Lewis the moment of prayer involves this awareness that what we ordinarily think of as the real world and the real "I" are facades. There is more behind them. There is a real and unknown "I" beyond the "I" who I imagine myself to be. "And in prayer this real I struggles to speak, for once from his real being, and to address, for once, not the other Actors, but—what shall I call Him?"[7]

In prayer one does not attempt to escape from space and time, or from the subject/object situation. Rather, one attempts to reawaken the awareness of just what that situation is. If that can be done, then every moment is a possible theophany. Thus Lewis says:

The prayer preceding all prayers is "May it be the real I who speaks. May it be the real Thou that I speak to." . . . Only God can reach this depth in us and only God can in mercy shatter every idea we form of Him. The most blessed result of prayer would be to rise thinking—"But I never before. I never dreamed . . ." I suppose it was at such a moment that Thomas Aquinas said of his own theology, "It reminds me of straw."[8]

Prayer—which for the simple believer is an uncomplicated matter of an I addressing a Thou, paralleling ordinary address on the interhuman level—for the intellectual presupposes an ontological understanding. To enter into prayer, into the presence of God, is to realize the distinction between appearance and reality, between the superficially real and the ultimately real, between creature and Creator.

If we understand the "prayer situation" in this fashion and see the implications for the way in which God relates to his world and human beings relate to God, at least some of the external criticisms of prayer and some of the Christian perplexities about prayer appear in a new light.

One of the questions skeptics raise about prayer when God is conceived of as omniscient is often put: Why tell God what he already knows? When God is also thought of as absolutely good, the further question is put: Why pray if God is all-knowing and all-good; will he not give you what is your good, in any case? Both of these arguments are met by what Lewis has described as the relation of God to the world. Prayer does add something in a sense to the knowledge of God. It doesn't add to what might be called the factual knowledge God has of us, but when we pray we are known in a new way or a different way—as persons who wish to be known. We are known as those who will to disclose themselves. This is a different kind of relationship which makes possible a good for us which otherwise would not be possible.

A second kind of issue is raised by those who believe that the world and its processes are determined. Prayer seems to them to require breaking a deterministic chain of causation and therefore must be rejected. Lewis' response is that even if determinism were the case, "every form of behaviour, including speech, can go on just the same and will." He seems to mean that, given a complete determinism, prayer becomes just as necessary as any other activity in nature and the human world. People will still necessarily act as if they had freedom. They "will still ask you to hand them the salt."[9]

As regards the view that human freedom requires a predictable world and that if God were to alter the course of events in answer to prayer it would destroy that predictability, Lewis answers that in any case we do not live in a predictable world. Planned and purposive action has always in fact been an expression of human freedom, especially in the face of an unknown future. Those who think that science aims at some ultimate predictability, Lewis thinks, misconceive what the sciences in fact do. The sciences predict, but only with respect to that in an event which is an instance of some universal law. They deliberately rule out the unique and particular. It is worth recalling here that Lewis conceives of God as relating himself concretely and immediately to each particular being and that he thinks Pope's view that ". . . the first Almighty Cause / Acts not by partial, but by general laws" would make prayer meaningless. "If there is a Providence at all, everything is providential and every providence is a special providence."[10]

For Lewis the problems that are critical are not those raised by the skeptics, e.g., how prayer can fit into a deterministic world view or how prayer makes any sense if God is omniscient, omnipotent, and all-good. If there is an adaptation between the free actions of men in prayer and the course of events, this is already inherent in God's creative act. It *is*, not "it has happened" or "it will happen." God and his acts are not in time. To human beings who are temporal it seems otherwise, but our prayers are heard before we make them, because both we and our prayers are in God's eternal creative act.[11]

Prayer and Causal Processes

The real problems for Lewis regarding prayer are theological, and they are problems raised by the believer. They have to do with how the relationship between divine and human action is to be understood, what kind of efficacy prayer may be said to have, and how prayer is to be related to the doctrine of the impassibility of God. Or they have to do with the apparent conflict between two contrasting views of prayer in the New Testament. The issues in the first group are interrelated. Can prayer be said to make any difference? Does prayer change the course of events? Does it change God or his actions in any way? "God," said Pascal, "instituted prayer in order to lend to His creatures

the dignity of causality." Is this true and, if so, in what
sense?

How indeed is prayer related to causal processes?
Does prayer have straightforward causal efficacy?
When a person prays that something will happen and
it does happen, does this mean that prayer caused it to
happen in some direct way? If that were true, the implication would be that the efficacy of prayer could be
tested in some empirical fashion. Prayer would be more
like magic, acting directly on nature and altering the
ongoing causal relations by adding some new factor.
Even the question, "Does prayer work?" suggests that
kind of frame of discussion. Such a viewpoint, Lewis
thinks, misleads us in our understanding of prayer. We
cannot establish empirically that we cause anything to
happen through prayer, and yet we do often see a connection between our prayer and a given event. We do
not believe that the connection is sheer coincidence.
Our sense of connection is analogous to that which we
see in human relationships where requests or proposals
are made. In a man's proposal of marriage what seems
to happen transcends any one-way causal relationship.
At the level of human requests we sometimes get what
we ask for and sometimes not. What we requested
might have happened anyway or the request may not
have initiated what we take to be a response. When we
feel assurance that our requests will be heard and responded to, the assurance does not come from scientific
knowledge but from knowing the persons involved. So
too with God. The relationship of making a request to
another human being is not a simple one-way causal
relationship paralleling our actions on things. This is
even truer in the case of our relationship to God in
prayer or at any other point of junction or separation
"where absolute being utters derivative being."[12] We
tend to assume that divine and human action exclude
each other. We must rather admit both that we are
agents and that God is involved in our agency. "We

have nothing that we have not received; but part of what we have received is the power of being more than receptacles."[13]

Of Pascal's statement that God "instituted prayer in order to allow His creatures the dignity of causality," Lewis writes that "it would perhaps be truer to say He invented both prayer and physical action for that purpose."[14] There is of course an important difference between work and prayer. In both we use the God-given agency and freedom to act in relation to that from which God's direct control has been withheld, but the kind of causality is different in each case. The causality we exercise in work is, one might say, divinely guaranteed. It is therefore ruthless. We can do as much harm as we please. Prayer is not like that. God retains a discretionary power. Otherwise we would destroy ourselves. Prayer is not a weaker form of causality but a stronger one. "When it 'works' at all, it works unlimited by space and time."[15] In either case there is a kind of divine abdication. We are both privileged and compelled to share in the process of creation. "Our act, when we pray, must not, any more than all our other acts, be separated from the continuous act of God Himself, in which alone all finite causes operate."[16]

Prayer then, unlike magic, is not direct action on nature. The human action of prayer cannot be conceived of apart from God's action, and somehow we believe that it acts on nature through God. Does this not mean that it acts on God, and if it acts on God, what then of the traditional notion of the impassibility of God? In a letter dated January 8, 1952, Lewis replies to a query:

But how can it change God's will? Well—but how v. odd it would be if God in His actions towards me were bound to ignore what I did (including my prayers). Surely He hasn't to forgive me for sins I didn't commit or to cure me of errors into which I have never fallen? In other words His will (however changeless in some ultimate metaphysical sense) must be related to what I am and do? And once grant that, and why should my asking or not asking not be *one* of the things He takes into account? At any rate He said he would—and he ought to know. (We often talk as if He were not very good at Theology!)[17]

Lewis returns to this subject in *Letters to Malcolm.* The fact that God forgives sins shows that "the divine action is consequent upon, conditioned by, elicited by our behaviour."[18] Whatever one means by impassibility and by action upon God must be interpreted in the light of such a conclusion. Scripture, Lewis says, takes no pains to "guard the doctrine of impassibility." Pascal's language implies a kind of direct causal power in prayer. It might be better to say that God takes into account all the situations produced by the acts of his creatures "before all worlds." "And if he takes our sins into account, why not our petitions?"[19] Language of this kind is more in keeping with the actual hopes and expectations Christians have regarding prayer: that God will hear, will take our prayers into account rather than that our prayer will somehow "cause" God to do our bidding.

The Efficacy of Prayer

A second theological problem for the believer arises in relation to two apparently conflicting patterns of petitionary prayer taught by the New Testament. This problem seems to have been of particular importance to Lewis himself, for he devoted a separate paper as well as a chapter of *Letters to Malcolm* to this issue and speaks of it as one of the "difficulties that really torment us."[20] The gist of the problem is that the New Testament and "the Lord Himself" teach us that all petitions are to be qualified by the clause "Thy will be done." This qualification Lewis thinks is not simply to be interpreted as submission. It may and ought to be also the

voice of joyful desire. We know too that Jesus' own
prayer in Gethsemane carried this same provision—
"Thy will be done"—and that it implied uncertainty
that his prayer would be granted. His prayer was in fact
not granted.

Contrasted with this is the other pattern of petitionary prayer in the New Testament. Whatever we ask for
in faith will be given to us. There is no demand for
submission of one's prayers to God's will and no uncertainty that the specific petitions will be granted. How,
asks Lewis, is this astonishing promise to be reconciled
with the Lord's Prayer and the Lord's example? How
is it to be reconciled with the observed fact that Christian prayers are often not granted, not only individual
prayers but explicit prayers in Christ's name by the
church itself? Lewis examines the New Testament texts
that embody this second pattern. He rejects the views
of those who would call the promises "archaisms" or
naive. He concludes that there is no satisfactory solution. He has only one suggestion—that the degree or
kind of faith required in the second pattern is one
which most believers never experience. Faith of the
kind referred to only appears "when the one who prays
does so as God's fellow-worker, demanding what is
needed for the joint work. At such moments the person
of faith is so united with God that something of the
divine foreknowledge enters his mind."[21] Yet one
might still ask: how does such an interpretation square
with Jesus' Gethsemane prayer? Lewis' answer is to
suggest that Jesus chose that night to plumb the depths
of Christian experience, to identify himself fully with
the weakest, or that in his Gethsemane prayer he "descends into the humiliation of being a suitor, praying on
his own behalf." When he does so, "the certitude about
His Father's will is apparently withdrawn."[22] As for us,
Lewis concludes, our struggle is not for faith in the
second sense. Our struggle is to believe that "God will

listen to our prayers, will take them into account." It is "even to go on believing that there is a Listener at all."[23]

While what we have been saying about Lewis' view of prayer up to this point refers to all prayer, it is particularly relevant to petitionary prayer. It is with prayers of petition that questions of the efficacy of prayer arise in their sharpest form. Lewis has the elderly devil, Screwtape, instruct Wormwood to raise difficulties about petitionary prayer:

Worry him with the haunting suspicion that the practice is absurd and can have no objective result. Don't forget to use the "heads I win, tails you lose" argument. If the thing he prays for doesn't happen, then that is one more proof that petitionary prayers don't work; if it does happen, he will of course be able to see some of the physical causes which led up to it, and "therefore it would have happened anyway," and thus a granted prayer becomes just as good a proof as a denied one that prayers are ineffective.[24]

Nevertheless, for Lewis, petitionary prayer alone does present problems for many people. In all its forms prayer is "either a sheer illusion or a personal contact between embryonic, incomplete person and the utterly concrete Person."[25]

Prayer in the sense of petition, asking for things, is a small part of it; confession and penitence are its threshold, adoration its sanctuary, the presence and vision and enjoyment of God its bread and wine. In it God shows Himself to us. That He answers prayer is a corollary—not necessarily the most important one—from that revelation. What He does is learned from what He is.[26]

Lewis writes more about petition and adoration than he does about confession and penitence as forms of prayer, but what he says about the latter is characteristically discriminating and concrete. On the one hand he wants to take real guilt and real feelings of guilt seriously. On the other he argues that either the pursuit of vague feelings of guilt or an overly scrupulous self-examination of conscience is not helpful in the Christian life. One needs self-knowledge, but not total self-knowledge. "I sometimes pray," he writes, "for just so much self-knowledge at the moment as I can bear and use at the moment; the little daily dose."[27] There are times too when we need to experience the wrath of God. Reality calls for penitential prayers, "acts" of penitence. To those who think this a crude anthropomorphic conception and a low level of prayer, Lewis would insist that the imagery of anger and indignation passing into an embracing re-welcoming love in reconciliation is true to personal relationship at the human level. It ensures that the prayer of confession and penitence is a genuine act and not simply a state of feeling. Nevertheless, Lewis believes that a continuous sense of one's own corruption and an ongoing self-scrutiny and cultivation of feelings of self-abhorrence is undesirable. Lewis believes, as his "devilish" remarks in Screwtape make clear, that prayer which concentrates on the inner life, on feelings and mood, on the "self," is a diversion of the fundamental outward movement of prayer, that prayer itself is this movement out from the self and is part of the basic pattern of salvation and sanctification which involves the loss of self to gain the self. Moreover, in prayer we turn toward the Creation and through the Creation to the Creator. That is why prayers should relate to real people, real actions in the world, rather than toward the cultivation of the inner spirit and so-called spiritual things. As Lewis puts it, "Our emotional reactions to our own behaviour are of limited ethical significance."[28]

ADORATION AND "PATCHES OF GODLIGHT"

Lewis' views of adoration are particularly interesting. As in so much of what he writes, he has a concern to have people make a beginning, and to begin where they are. Out of his own conversion experience, he

seems to have a pastoral sense that neither the non-
believers nor the believers need all start at the same
place or at the same level. One does not in adoration
have to start by "summoning up" the whole "goodness
and greatness of God." One does not have to begin by
thinking about creation and redemption and "all the
blessings of this life."[29] Rather, Lewis advises, one
might begin with the particular pleasures we experience in Nature. "Pleasures are shafts of the glory as it
strikes our sensibility."[30] It is not nature as a whole, but
the beauty of a flower, the sound of the wind, the taste
of an apple which are beginning points. Such pleasures
can be turned into channels of adoration not simply by
giving thanks for them but by receiving them and
recognizing their divine source in a single experience
—that is, not by first having the experiencing and then
interpreting it. To experience such a tiny theophany is
in fact adoration. Gratitude says: "Thank you. How
good God is to give me this." Adoration says: "What
must be the quality of that Being whose far off and
momentary coruscations are like this!"[31] If one could
respond in this fashion, every experience might be a
channel of adoration. Inattention or the wrong kind of
attention or what Lewis calls the demand for an "en-
core" of some past joy, rather than attending to the
possibility of the present moment, keep us from achiev-
ing what we might. Lewis believes that adoration in
this sense is not only good in itself. Through it we are
enabled to adore God on the highest occasions, if we
have learned the habit of doing so on these small occasions. We may know and believe that God is adorable,
but we will not have found him so apart from such
experience.

Even more important in a sense, these "patches of
Godlight" in the woods of our experience have for
Lewis an eschatological significance. God is certainly
the Tragic Redeemer, perhaps even a Tragic Creator in

that something of the tragic may be inherent in every act of creation, but *finally,* that is in the *end,* images like play and dance convey the meaning of life for the blessed. Not the notion of frivolity but that of joy is the clue. The End, for Lewis, is to be "utterly spontaneous, to be the complete reconciliation of boundless freedom with order, with the most delicately adjustive, supple, intricate and beautiful order." The image is the dance and "Joy is the serious business of Heaven."[32]

THE RELATION OF CREATOR TO CREATURE

What Lewis has to say about adoration and the "patches of Godlight" points to the large significance he gives to the doctrine of Creation for the Christian's understanding of prayer and for a Christian apologetic. God is incommensurable with man and with the world, says Lewis. There is an unimaginable distinction between them. The Creator is different from the creature in a way that must be radically distinguished from the way in which creatures differ from each other. Though Lewis rejects pantheism, he believes that God is in each of his created beings as they can never be in one another. He is in each of them as the ground of their being, as the ground and root and continual supply of their reality. "Therefore of each creature we can say, 'this also is Thou: neither is this Thou.' "[33] The presence of God in particular objects is not quite what many would mean by omnipresence, which may carry with it some suggestion of spatial extension. God is present in each thing, but not necessarily in the same mode. "The higher the creature, the more, and also the less, God is in it; the more present by grace and the less present (by a sort of abdication) as mere power.[34] Thus the ontological continuity between the Creator and all creatures must be distinguished "from the union of wills which, under grace, is reached by a life of sanctity."[35] It is

toward such union and sanctity that prayer aims. It is
not necessary to leave the creatures behind to find God.
"He walks everywhere incognito."[36]

Something of this view of the relationship of the Creator to the creature is reflected in Lewis' response to
the charge that prayer may simply be soliloquy, man
talking to himself. In one sense Lewis agrees. Prayer is,
in its most perfect state, soliloquy. "If the Holy Spirit
speaks in the man, then in prayer God speaks to God.
... 'God did (or said) it' and 'I did (or said) it,' can both
be true. ... The deeper the level within ourselves from
which our prayer, or any other act, wells up, the more
it is His, but not at all the less ours. Rather, most ours
when most His. ... To be discontinuous from God as I
am discontinuous from you would be annihilation."[37]

Lewis does not write much about intercessory
prayer, but it is clear from his letters and from the
memories of those who knew him that intercession was
a regular practice for him and that he often sought the
intercession of others.[38] He says at one point that intercession may be easier than prayers that have to do with
the self, since in prayer relating to oneself one has to do
something about it. Nor does Lewis offer any special
theological grounding for intercessory prayer distinct
from that of his understanding of the relation of God to
human existence and to time. God "takes account" of
all that is and all that happens, including human
prayers. It is something of this same background which
must be understood if we are to grasp what Lewis says
about prayer for the dead. To most Protestants, Lewis'
views on prayer for the dead will seem odd, for they
seem to carry with them some notion like that of purgatory. Indeed, so they do for Lewis. His point is simple.
If we pray for the living, why not for the dead? After
all, the dead include those who were and are dearest to
us. And if we eliminate the distortions emphasizing
retributive punishment rather than purification, the
idea of purgatory seems to be required, Lewis thinks,

even by our own feelings about ourselves and our needs. To those who would say that the dead are not in time, Lewis responds that it seems to him better to think that they are in time, though time and the relation to God are experienced in a different fashion among them than among the living. They are certainly not to be thought of as eternal in the sense that God is. To think of the blessed dead as strictly timeless would be inconsistent with the notion of the resurrection of the body. If we can pray for the dead, ought we to ask the dead, especially the saints, to pray for us, as some traditions advocate? Lewis sees dangers in this, but he asks, "Who am I to judge the practices of others?"[39] On the other hand, to pray with rather than to the saints is, he thinks, a good thing. Here if one unites "one's own little twitter with the voice of the great saints and (we hope) of our own dear dead, we may find that our own prayers become richer and some of their uglier qualities diminished."[40]

PRACTICAL MATTERS

Much of what Lewis wrote about prayer was theological, attempting to answer the skeptics or clear up difficulties for Christian believers. *Letters to Malcolm* and his actual letters to correspondents also contain something of his views on the practice of prayer. The general impression this material makes is of one who was tolerant of the inclinations and practices of others but who had definite preferences of his own that he was willing to share. Lewis discusses the issue of using formal written prayers versus using one's own words or praying without words. He himself preferred expressing his prayers in his own language, but he thought that when one was at one's best, one's prayers really do not require words. At its height prayer may be "beyond words," yet words serve to focus and to channel thoughts. Using one's own words keeps prayer in touch

with one's unique situation. Formal prayers have their
uses too. They keep one in touch with the faith of the
church, reminding one of what one ought to ask for,
and adding a ceremonial note.

Lewis believed that one should feel free to pray any-
where and anytime (though he thought bedtime prayer
unproductive). His friends have reported that he said
his own prayers while traveling by train between Oxford and Cambridge, or pacing up and down in the
driveway after visiting his wife in a nursing home, or at
the end of the afternoon, and just before dinner.[41]
Whether one should kneel or not was not important to
him, but he felt prayer demanded concentration of
mind and body. Under some conditions kneeling is appropriate, at others sitting or standing. In prayer one
should begin where one is, bringing what *is* in us before
God, not what ought to be in us. If we do not turn to
God in small things, Lewis says, we may not in the
important ones either. Lewis recognizes that we may
be reluctant to pray, that prayer may seem irksome to
us. He knew that it is difficult to keep what is concrete
but immaterial before us. In Screwtape's advice to
Wormwood, Lewis points to one of the difficulties we
humans have in praying and has Screwtape suggest
how the "devil" can make the most of it. He speaks of
the difficulty that human beings have (in contrast to the
devils) in envisioning God as they pray. What one
would find if one looked within the mind of the one at
prayer is "a composite object containing many quite
ridiculous ingredients." The composite may include
New Testament images, bodily sensations objectified
and attributed to the object revered, "God" located at
the corner of the bedroom ceiling, or in a crucifix on the
wall, etc. The point, says Screwtape, is to keep the
human praying to it—to the thing he has made, "not to
the Person who has made him." The danger is that the
one who prays may come to make the distinction, says
Screwtape, "not to what I think thou art but to what

thou knowest thyself to be." Then the one who prays will fling aside his own thoughts and images, or at least recognize their merely subjective nature, and trust himself to "the completely real, external, invisible Presence, there with him in the room and never knowable by him as he is known by it." This is the real nakedness of the soul in prayer which the devil must prevent at all costs.[42] Lewis says that even these difficulties should be taken up in one's prayers. In any case he believes it is no good "angling for rich moments." God speaks to us most intimately when we are "off guard."[43] Sometimes what we feel are our worst prayers may be in God's eyes our best.

One of Lewis' most interesting reports about his own personal practice of prayer brings together the power and richness of formal prayer of the church's tradition and the personal uniqueness and relevance characteristic of extempore prayer in one's own words. This he calls "festooning." "Festoons" are the private grace notes which Lewis said he liked to hang on the basic petitions of the Lord's Prayer. They are a kind of personalization and particularization of the petitions. "Festoons" are a way of giving specific and particular relevance to what might otherwise simply be an abstract, general, and traditional form.

THE LANGUAGE OF FAITH AND PRAYER

What C. S. Lewis writes about the theology of prayer and about his own practice of prayer looks like a sophisticated version of what is preached in the marketplace as evangelical Christianity. Indeed Lewis has been claimed by those who think of themselves as theological conservatives, as orthodox and antiliberal. His avowed supernaturalism, his repudiation of the demythologizers, his acceptance of the traditional doctrines of heaven, hell, angels, miracles, and the rest, seems to support such claims. Interpreted wholly within such a framework Lewis would, I think, be misunderstood. The greater complexity of Lewis' thought can be disclosed if we attend to what he says about language, the language we use to talk about the substance of the Christian faith, and the language of prayer itself. Time and again Lewis contrasts the anthropomorphic language of the Bible and of common Christian speech with the abstractions of theology and philosophy. He says that we should never think that the anthropomorphic images are a concession to our weakness and that the abstractions are the literal truth. Both are concessions. Each taken alone is in some sense false. Together they correct one another. Or again, he says that our language in talking about God is analogical. We must not think that we can get rid of analogy and put a theological abstraction in its place. The value of the abstraction is that it keeps us from making prosaic extrapolations from the analogical expressions. Never take the images literally, says Lewis, and when their purport for our existence seems to contrast with the theological abstractions, trust the images. So too, we should distrust demythologizing. Lewis thinks that often demythologizing is only a remythologization—a substitution of a poorer mythology for a richer one.

As early as 1932 Lewis was pointing to this contrast between the particularity and power of language in its first stage, where words seem to burst with meaning, and the final stage, where they are admirably clear but one is so far away from real things that they really say nothing. He writes:

Compare "Our Father which art in Heaven" with "The supreme being transcends space and time." The first goes to pieces if you begin to apply the literal meaning to it. . . . The second falls into no such traps. On the other hand the first really means something, really represents a concrete experience in the minds of those who use it; the second is mere dexterous playing with counters.[44]

What Lewis seems to be saying clearly and then demonstrating in his own religious writing is that there is a primary language—concrete, analogical, anthropomorphic, mythopoetic—which carries the existential understanding of the meaning of human experience and of the reality which grounds that experiencing. One cannot get behind the language or reduce it without losing the reality and the experience which is shared through it. We come to see by means of this primary language. It is the means by which reality at its depth dimension comes to be for us. Theology, theory, abstract notions, doctrines as such, are not to be rejected or disregarded, but they cannot replace the primary concrete language of the Christian community which grew out of and expressed that mode of consciousness in which Christians expressed and shared the gospel. The Christian story is like a myth. In one sense —when one understands Lewis' high evaluation of the mythopoetic—it is myth. But, for Lewis, it is myth that has become a fact. What Lewis is asserting is that primary Christian language, and the story it embodies, really does re-present, embody, incarnate, the reality that we call God. If we are to be found by or to discover this unimaginable reality, we can do it through coming to share this language and this story. Though what Lewis writes appears to be rational argument, critical apologetics, and the like, in some ways it gains its power and perhaps its popular appeal because it is even more fundamentally *testimony.* It has the authority of someone who has found something out and who tells us, not how he feels, but how things are.

7

Thomas Merton—
Theology of Contemplation

THOMAS MERTON (1915–1968) was a Trappist monk
whose conversion to Catholicism was told in *The Seven
Storey Mountain.* Merton's writings on prayer and
spirituality have made him America's most widely read
Catholic writer. Merton moved from a traditional Catholic contemplative life to prophetic involvement in the
issues of the 1960's and to dialogue with the spiritual
traditions of the East. *Contemplative Prayer* and *Zen
and the Birds of Appetite* are two representative books.

For Thomas Merton the goal of human life is union
with God, a process in which we take on the form of
Christ and become new beings in both our personal and
our social existence. Prayer is the path that can lead to
new being, to union with God. For Merton there are
two basic forms of prayer: infused prayer and ordinary
prayer. Infused prayer is a gift. The one who prays
cannot "cause" it, though it must be *actively* received.
Merton calls this contemplation in the strict sense. Ordinary prayer, or what Merton calls *active contemplation,* includes all the traditional practices of the interior
life—vocal prayer, meditation, mental or silent prayer,
liturgical prayer, spiritual or devotional reading, meditational labor. Such prayer prepares the way for love.
It teaches obedience and humility. Infused prayer, or
contemplation in the narrow sense, is not for everyone,
though everyone can desire the gift and pray for it.

Ordinary prayer is in practice, if not in theory, *absolutely essential to a truly Christian life.*[1]

MYSTICAL OR INFUSED PRAYER

In its strict sense, writes Merton, "contemplation is a supernatural love and knowledge of God, simple and obscure, infused by Him into the summit of the soul, giving it direct and experimental contact with Him." It is "an intuition of God born of pure love." As a gift "it transcends all the natural capacities of the soul." Nevertheless, it is both a human action and an action of God. It is "an intellectual experience of the fact that God is infinite love, that He has given Himself to us, and that from henceforth, love is all that matters."[2] At the same time that it is a human action or experience, the love with which one loves God comes from God. Since one's whole being is reconstituted as new being in mystical or infused prayer, one might say that such prayer is a new mode of existence.

ORDINARY PRAYER—ACTIVE CONTEMPLATION

Active contemplation or ordinary prayer is what "man" does. It may stop short of mystical prayer or it may be a preparation for it. It operates on the natural level, aided by ordinary grace. The function of active contemplation is "to awaken and prepare the mind, to turn the heart towards God, to arouse a desire to know God better and to rest in him. . . . Above all . . . [it] prepares the way for love."[3] These two forms of prayer, contemplation in the strict sense and ordinary prayer (or active contemplation), do not exhaust the possibilities leading to union with God. Some will come to union with God through action. If one lives for God and His love alone, this is a kind of quasi or masked contemplation. Such persons may achieve purity of heart through "obedience, fraternal charity, self-sacrifice and perfect abandonment to God's will in all that they do and suffer," even though they may never rise above the "ordinary levels of vocal or affective prayer."[4]

MOVEMENT TOWARD MYSTICAL PRAYER

The meaning of mystical prayer is more clearly understood in the light of the movement toward its actualization. The movement is one that involves the transformation of the self. For Merton there is a fundamental contrast between the true self and the false self. He develops this contrast further through his use of other terms: inner/outer, transcendent/empirical, deeper/superficial, full/empty, God-centered/self-centered. The true self is the real "I," the image of God, pure consciousness in contrast to the self or the "I" that is presupposed in the subject/object split, which Merton sometimes calls the Cartesian self or the "I," or the alienated self in contrast to the authentic self.

Merton's point is that there is a radical difference between the self as it is under the conditions of existence and the self as it really is, as it is meant to be, as it will be when it is properly related to God through mystical prayer in union with God. Again and again Merton declares that each of us is to be the self he or she really is, i.e., the self in union with God, the self whose center is not itself, but God. Traditional Christian teaching is that human beings are fallen. They are sinners. Merton interprets the Fall as a fall from unity into multiplicity. The self is separated from God, and this separation means turning the world and the self into objects. This split between subject and object must be transcended or healed. Cartesian consciousness must be overcome. For Merton, no technique can accomplish this. If the inner self is to be released,

all that we can do with any spiritual discipline is produce within ourselves something of the silence, the humility, the detachment, the purity of heart and the indifference which are required if the inner self is to make some shy, unpredictable manifestation of his presence.[5]

Merton's doctrine of the false self is then a contemporary interpretation of the doctrine of sin.[6] The alienation of the self from God is the self's perverse attachment to itself, to itself apart from God, as if the self apart from God is real. Such a self is not real; it is illusory. Living as if one is an independent self is living a constant lie. It is this condition which underlies contemporary doubt and self-questioning, the existential dread which is experienced as a sense of insecurity, lostness, exile, emptiness, boredom, disorientation.

Union with God comes through a reconstitution of the self and the sense of self. The false self must be replaced by the true self. Sometimes Merton speaks of this process as a battle:

It is the battle of our own strength, lodged in the exterior self, with the strength of God which is the life and actuality of our interior self. . . . This power is more than our own strength, it is the power of love, and it secretly comes from within, from the antagonist Himself.[7]

What contemplation is all about is this battle. One must come to see the nothingness of oneself apart from God. One does this by stripping away the layers of the false self until one finds "one's deepest center," where one is one with God by virtue of God's own love.[8] We come to know God insofar as we become aware of ourselves as known.[9] Self-knowledge and the knowledge of God are inextricably tied together, but it is knowledge of the true self as known by God which brings union with God. It is the false self which obstructs our knowledge of being known by God. What contemplation helps to make possible is an inner revolution in self-understanding, involving a process of purification that strips us to the point of realizing our nothingness. Paradoxically, as we realize our nothingness, our utter emptiness, we are given fullness. We become aware of ultimacy, of new being, of oneness with God. One must lose one's self (the false, superficial self) in order to find one's self (the self as given by, and in communion with, God).[10]

For one moving toward mystical union (in Merton's writing, normally the monk), prayer, reading, and meditation are inseparable. Together they are a way of finding—or better, of being found—by God and a way of "resting in him whom we have found." Prayer of this kind is a "prayer of silence, simplicity, contemplative and meditative unity, a deep personal integration in an attentive, watchful listening of 'the heart,' . . . a wordless and total surrender of the heart in silence."[11]

When Merton writes in this way of prayer of the heart, he is saying that such prayer involves the whole person (not just the mind or the affections) and that it comes from one's deepest center. It comes from the depths of our being, "where self-awareness goes beyond analytical reflection and opens out into metaphysical and theological confrontation with the abyss of the unknown—yet present—one."[12] Such prayer transcends and includes the apparent divisions between mental and vocal prayer, public and private prayer, and centers "the entire day's activities in an organic whole."[13]

There are methods and techniques of praying and meditating, but more important than these is the cultivation of an attitude or outlook of "faith, openness, attention, reverence, expectation, supplication, trust, joy."[14] These come to permeate our being with love as our faith "tells us we are in the presence of God, that we live in Christ, that in the Spirit of God we 'see' God our Father without 'seeing.' We know him in 'unknowing.' "[15]

There is movement in meditation, an alternation from darkness to light. We descend into "our own nothingness, a recognition of helplessness, frustration, infidelity, confusion, ignorance." Then, out of the profound distress in our nothingness and total need of God, he "draws us out of darkness into light." He "hears us, answers our prayer, recognizes our need, and grants us the help we require." This help may be only the gift of more faith that "he can and will help us in his own time."[16] Effort is necessary for such movement. It must be enlightened, sustained, and well directed. For this reason, Merton believes a spiritual director is needed at this level of prayer and meditation. We need to have someone who can help us recognize the action of God in relation to our prayer, someone who can show us how to be humble and patient, how to develop insight into our difficulties, and how to remove the obstacles to deepening our life of prayer.

It is clear from Merton's numerous writings that there are serious obstacles to progress in prayer. One such obstacle is that we do not want to be beginners. Therefore we are not really teachable, not really open to learning what we must learn if we are to move ahead. A second obstacle is spiritual inertia, inner confusion, coldness, lack of confidence. This obstacle is likely to appear after a real beginning has been made. Concentration becomes difficult. The feelings and imagination wander or run wild. One's inner life becomes dry and dulled. Merton suggests that this difficulty is serious. It may be the result of separating the interior life from the concrete realities of everyday life, as if there were a cleavage between the inner life and the rest of existence, or as if the supernatural were totally separated from nature and life.

A somewhat similar obstacle develops when people turn their meditation inward in such a way as to close themselves off from others. The openness to and love of others should be a stimulus to our interior life. Meditation that does focus on the interior life should nevertheless not wall the self off or bring one to a kind of defensive or self-centered absorption in one's own self. Other obstacles Merton mentions are discouragement, confusion, and a sense of helplessness. In all these cases the remedy is not a technique, but a simple turning to God in the realization that the Spirit "is given to us, wholly, in Christ. That he prays in us when we do not know how to pray." This is the function of meditation, through the increasing realization of our utter dependence on grace "to bring us to this attitude of awareness and receptivity."[17]

An obstacle of a different order is not treated extensively in Merton's published writings on the spiritual life, but it can be read between the lines in his diaries and letters and explicitly in his unpublished work "Inner Experience." It is clear that Merton believed, and knew from his own experience, that ascetic practices themselves can stand in the way of movement in prayer. He writes of those who turn the religious life "into a procrustean bed on which potential saints and contemplatives have been so pulled apart and crippled that they have ended their lives as freaks." He speaks of the contemplative who, even though not expressly forbidden to follow what he believes to be the inspiration of God, "may feel himself continually and completely at odds with the accepted ideals of those around him." He writes vividly:

Their spiritual exercises may seem to him to be a bore and a waste of time. Their sermons and their conversation may leave him exhausted with a sense of futility. . . . Their choral offices, their excitement over liturgical ceremony and chant, may rob him of the delicate taste of an interior manna that is not found in formulas of prayer and exterior rites. If only he could be alone and quiet, and remain in the emptiness, darkness and purposelessness in which God speaks with such overwhelming effect.[18]

One senses in this comment much of what may have led Merton himself to seek more and more solitude and finally to become a hermit.

If the obstacles can be managed, one passes from meditation, understood as active mental prayer, to contemplation in the sense of a "deeper and simpler intuitive form of receptivity, in which if one can be said to 'meditate' at all, one does so only by receiving the light with passive and loving attention."[19] Thus the goal of monastic prayer, including psalmody, active mental prayer, meditation in the sense of prayer of the heart, and even devotional reading is "to prepare the way so that God's action may develop this 'faculty for the supernatural,' this capacity for inner illumination by faith and by the light of wisdom, in the loving contemplation of God."[20] Such illumination can take place only where there is purity of heart, "an unconditional and totally humble surrender to God, a total acceptance of ourselves and of our situation as willed by Him."[21] Purity of heart is the correlative of the new identity, the new being.

Merton's view of the way to purity of heart shows a clear resemblance to that of traditional mystical theology. The quest for God is evoked by an awakened consciousness of emptiness. It moves through the dying of the self, through dread, through the dark night to the illumination that is beyond understanding, the knowing that is an unknowing. Meditation, says Merton, should begin with the realization of our own nothingness and helplessness, a coming to the recognition that our "external everyday self is to a great extent a mask and a fabrication, that the very idea of a separate individual self is an illusion."[22] Since we must learn to receive grace wherever God may grant it, we must develop a "permanent disposition to humility, attention to reality, receptivity, pliability." To do this requires getting free "from habitual hardness of heart, torpor and grossness of mind, due to arrogance and nonacceptance of simple reality, or resistance to the concrete demands of God's will."[23] We must learn to control our thoughts and desires, to detach ourselves from inordinate cares. Such efforts involve the use or the sacrifice of all created things in the interest of love. If there is no sacrifice, there will be no prayer, and vice versa.

But meditation will involve more than sacrifice. Those who seek illumination and union will pass through dry places and through the experience of dread. We become weary; "thought becomes difficult and even impossible, and the imagination no longer obeys our will and desires."[24] We become anxious. We come to realize in experience that we cannot control our inner life, and this realization is a step toward giving up our effort to control, to leave everything to God. We may begin to abandon our defenses the more we realize that we are in fact defenseless. Merton sees these conscious efforts to control as our defenses against unconscious forces, defenses which are also limitations. Yet as we give up the defenses we enter into the unknown, into a darkness where "all spiritual light is darkened, all values lose their shape and reality, and we remain, so to speak, suspended in the void."[25]

At this point we are at the crucial juncture of our experience of darkness. We are tempted to doubt God himself. Until this point our mind grasped God "in simple and primitive images." Now we enter the "night in which he is present without any image, invisible, inscrutable, and beyond any satisfactory mental representation."[26] Merton describes what may happen to prayer under such conditions:

Prayer may become an obscure and hateful struggle to preserve the images and trappings which covered his own interior emptiness. Either he will have to face the truth of his emptiness or else he will beat a retreat into the realm of images and analogies which no longer serve for a more spiritual life.[27]

Not everyone can face "the terrible experience of being apparently without faith in order to really grow in faith," yet this purgation must take place in order to eliminate the human and accidental elements of faith and liberate the spiritual power in the center of our being.[28] Merton quotes St. John of the Cross, who says that the soul must be blinded and darkened so that it will depend on "none of the things he understands, experiences, feels and imagines." Faith is "above all that he understands, experiences, feels and imagines,"[29] an illumination that escapes the investigation and control of the understanding. It is the uncomprehensible, the "pure, unknowable, ineffable and mysterious good which is God."[30]

We cannot in this experience grasp God as an object that can be comprehended by our minds. We must transcend ourselves and our analogies. We must transcend the subject/object character of ordinary knowing.

Instead we know him in so far as we become aware of ourselves as known through and through by him. . . . Our knowledge of God is paradoxically a knowledge not of him as the object of our scrutiny, but *of ourselves* as utterly dependent on his saving and merciful knowledge of us. It is in proportion as we are known to him that we find our real being and identity in Christ.[31]

This experience or intuition of God is a knowing through an unknowing. "Only when we are able to 'let go' of everything within us, all desire to see, to know, to taste and to experience the presence of God, do we truly become able to experience that presence with the overwhelming conviction and reality that revolutionize our entire inner life."[32]

From what Merton writes, it is clear that the fullness of the life of the spirit can only come when one passes through dread and anguish, through the dark night and death of the self-centered self. The personal experience of emptiness, of aridity, of a kind of internal hell are necessary and inescapable dimensions of contemplative prayer. But how can one be sure that such experiences indicate that real contemplation is occurring? For as Merton says, such experiences can also be the result of sin, infidelity, laziness, or even bad health. Merton answers that there are certain signs for the reality of infused contemplation even in the midst of the dread and the emptiness. One sign is that one continues to seek in spite of the apparent hopelessness; another is the forgetfulness of ordinary cares and of the routine level of life in the darkness of prayer. A third sign is that there is always something positive in the experience no matter how negative it may at first seem. Merton writes:

The surest sign of infused contemplation behind the cloud of darkness is a *powerful, mysterious and yet simple attraction which holds the soul prisoner in this darkness and obscurity.* Although the soul is filled with a sense of affliction and defeat, *it has no desire to escape from this aridity. . . .* All created goods only make it restless. They cannot satisfy it. *But at the same time there is a growing conviction that joy and peace and fulfilment are only to be found somewhere in this lonely night of aridity and faith.* [33]

The Experience of Mystical Union

And then suddenly, suddenly comes the awakening. "The soul has entered a new world." Unexpectedly and surprisingly, in the darkness it has found the living God. It is overpowered by the sense that God's love surrounds it. "Nothing else matters. The darkness remains as dark as ever and yet, somehow, it seems to have become brighter than the brightest day." Now the soul's interior life is completely simple. "It consists of one thought, one love, GOD ALONE." This, says Merton, drawing upon St. Bernard, is a pure and simple love which draws and absorbs "every other activity of the soul to itself. . . . This love infused into the soul by God unifies all its powers and raises them up to Him, separating its desires and affections more and more from the world and from perishing things. . . . [The soul] has no eyes for anything or anyone but God alone."[34] This infusion of love marks the entrance into the maturity of spiritual life, the illuminative way, and indicates that the movement is toward complete union with

God, drawn by God's own love. There is more to be said about this movement and its culmination. Merton sheds light on it especially when he explores the analogies and similarities between Christian and Eastern experience.

ORDINARY PRAYER

Contemplative prayer and the contemplative life represent the highest form of prayer and of the life of spirit. Other forms of prayer are not, however, rejected or to be diminished in importance. On the one hand, not everyone is temperamentally fitted or called to contemplation in the strict sense. On the other, noncontemplative forms of prayer may be stages preparatory to mystical or infused prayer. We turn therefore to Merton's views on meditation, liturgical prayer, vocal prayer, etc.

In its broadest sense meditation is reflection, a kind of directed concentrated attention. Religious reflection involves more than the mind. It involves the whole being. It is a kind of thinking united to love in which one enters into and knows from within the reality upon which one is meditating. One tries to absorb what one has already taken in. Meditation is not content with knowledge about. It wants direct knowledge. Yet meditation is still primarily a matter of thought, though it is the beginning of the interior prayer leading to the unitive and loving knowledge that is true contemplation.

Meditation has two kinds of goals. The immediate purpose may be the understanding of a particular truth or the resolution of a particular problem, but the ultimate end is communion with God. For example, one may (and should) meditate on the Bible, particularly on the Psalms, the mystery of Christ's sacrifice, and the Eucharist, or on Christ's patience so that one may practice patience, but in such meditation there is more at stake. One becomes identified with Christ and is led to a mystical participation in Christ's passion and death. In this way one comes to realize in consciousness the "union that is already truly effected between our souls and God by grace."[35]

In order to meditate properly we must withdraw our minds from what diverts us from God. We must recollect our senses, that is, withdraw our interest and desires from whatever is not useful or necessary to our interior life. We must have a sense of our own indigence, of our spiritual poverty, of the lack of what we seek. We are like the prodigal son, in exile and in spiritual need. Trials and temptations may help us realize our needs. We must have an atmosphere favorable to meditation—silence, tranquillity, recollection, and peace. We cannot hope to pray well if we are overcome by external activities. For some, however, prayer may be combined with work.

The aim of mental prayer is to awaken the Holy Spirit within us, to let him speak and pray within us. To do this we must be utterly sincere, never saying anything "we do not really mean, or at least sincerely intend to mean."[36] We must be "honest to God." Meditation should have focus and unity, moving toward "the emergence of one dominant attraction—a concentration of the interior life on one objective, union with God."[37] We are helped in this direction if our meditation has a definite, concrete, personal subject related to some mystery of the Christian faith. We begin with the mystery perceived externally as it has been experienced generation after generation in the church. Our senses and imagination, our emotions, feelings, affections are all involved in grasping the mystery. But then we must seek to "read the inner meaning beneath the surface . . . and to *relate the historical events given us in the Gospels with our own spiritual life here and now.*"[38] The goal is "to *realize* and to *actualize* in our own experience the fundamental truths of our faith."[39]

Sometimes we need to meditate directly on issues

and problems in our own lives and events in the history of our time. Merton says, for example, that a person who has meditated on the Passion of Christ but not on Dachau and Auschwitz has not yet fully entered into contemporary Christian experience. For understanding either trivial or important events it is important to bring a religious perspective to these events. Our own death and judgment and the Passion, death, and resurrection of Christ joined to such events can bring such a perspective.

Meditation is a work of love and desire. Its intent is to awaken our interior self, attuning it to the Holy Spirit so that we can respond to his grace, and in self-renunciation be brought to abandonment to the will and action of God. Merton outlines the essentials of meditative prayer in schematic form:

(1) *Preliminary:* A sincere effort of recollection, a realization of what you are about to do, and a prayer of petition for grace. If this beginning is well made, the rest ought to follow easily.

(2) *Vision:* The attempt to see, to focus, to grasp what you are meditating on. This implies an effort of *faith.* Keep working until faith is clear and firm in your heart (not merely in your head).

(3) *Aspiration:* From what you "see" there follow certain practical consequences. Desires, resolutions to act in accordance with one's faith, to live one's faith. Here, an effort of *hope* is required—one must believe in the *possibility* of these good acts, one must hope in the fulfilment of good desires, with the help of God. Above all, one must have a sincere hope in the possibility of divine union.

(4) *Communion:* Here the prayer becomes simple and uncomplicated. The realization of faith is solid, hope is firm, one can rest in the presence of God. This is more a matter of simple repose and intuition, an embrace of simple *love.* But if activity is required, let love have an active character, in which case the prayer is more like the last level (3). Or love may take rather the form of *listening* to the Beloved. Or the form of *praise.* More often than not, we can be content to simply rest, and float peacefully with the deep current of love, doing nothing of ourselves, but allowing the Holy Spirit

to act in the secret depths of our souls. If the prayer becomes confused or weak, we can return to one of the earlier stages, and renew our vigilance, our faith, our love.

We can end up with a brief and sincere prayer of thanksgiving.[40]

We have outlined the essentials of meditation according to Merton and of the contemplation that is its goal. Characteristically both meditation and contemplation are silent, silent in the sense that they are not vocal, but also in the deeper sense that ultimately in contemplation there is an interior silence, a wordless listening, a completely receptive attention. This silence has its own power. Merton quotes the desert father Ammonas: "It is by silence that the saints grew. . . . It was because of silence that the power of God dwelt in them. [It was] because of silence that the mysteries of God were known to them."[41] To the reader of Merton's journals it is clear that his views of the significance of silence grew out of his own experience as well as out of the traditional teachings of the contemplatives. Part of the tension between being a monk and being a writer centered in his awareness of the conflict between speech and silence. Part of it also was a reflection of his sense of the inability of words to encompass the mystery of God and of God's relation to human existence. But more particularly his appreciation of the importance of silence, both internal and external, is grounded in his sense that all distraction, all of the self—the false empirical self—including finally its language and its speech, must be put aside so that the self does not put itself between the real self and God. God gives and God's own language is silence. Finally the interior silence of prayer has to be utterly simple and beyond words, perhaps even beyond thoughts. Prayer that consists of "busy discursive acts," or logical reasoning, active imagining, and the deliberate stirring up of affections can get in the way of the receptive attention to the inner working of the Holy Spirit. Ultimately we should come to a "wordless and total surrender of the heart in silence."[42] Such silence is also related by Merton to the traditional notion of continual prayer. It may of course be possible to recite the psalms or some verbal formulae continuously as one works or carries on one's life, but it is even more possible to cultivate an ongoing attitude of attention that is silent and pervasive of one's whole life.[43]

Other forms of ordinary prayer such as individual vocal prayer and liturgical prayer receive less attention, though they have their place and importance in Merton's thought. In one sense we can attribute this lack of emphasis to Merton's assumption that such prayer was important for the life of the individual Christian and for the church and that it would continue. In another sense we can attribute it to his understanding that such prayer was instrumental to the realization of the ultimate goal of all prayer which is best disclosed in mystical or infused prayer and that finally silence, in which the Holy Spirit works and God's love brings new being, must overcome the speaking of human beings. Nor is much said by Merton about that form of vocal prayer which is so central to many other writers, petition. Merton's general stance is that prayer should not be directed toward ulterior purposes. The mark of the contemplative orientation in prayer is its uselessness, its purity. He writes that when prayer becomes busy and filled with ulterior purposes or is committed to programs beneath its own level it loses its true character.[44] This does not mean that we can never pray "for particular goods." Petitionary prayer may be compatible with the spirit of contemplation. In fact, we must petition God, *"but when prayer allows itself to be exploited* for purposes which are beneath itself and have nothing directly to do with our life in God, . . . then it becomes strictly impure."[45] For Merton, celebration and praise that involve loving attention to the presence of God are more important than asking for and getting "things." If we seek the Kingdom first, then all the rest comes along with it.

Merton has more to say about liturgical and corporate prayer, but, as we have indicated, there appears to be some tension in his own experience and thought concerning liturgical prayer. Nevertheless, at many points he writes of the great significance of liturgical prayer. Liturgical prayer teaches active contemplation by its theological and biblical content and through its art, music, and poetry. Its central action, the Mass, helps bring the contemplative to participation in Christ's divine Sonship. The Sacrament is not simply a symbol for contemplation. "It contains Him who is the beginning and end of all contemplation."[46] Liturgy may be said to extend itself into personal prayer, and personal prayer "seeks fulfillment in liturgical worship."[47] So too the prayer of the individual and the prayer of the community are inextricably tied together. The working and praying community is the supportive context in which the life of prayer develops. Yet Merton could write of his own experience in *The Sign of Jonas:*

As soon as I get to choir I am overwhelmed by distractions. No sense of anything except difficulty and struggle and pain. Objectively speaking I suppose it is more perfect to thank God through the liturgy. The choral office should be the best way of continuing one's Communion. For me it is the worst.[48]

Teahan has attributed this ambivalence to Merton's personality—to the simultaneous attraction to solitude and a strong need for companionship.[49] Perhaps this is the case, but it seems likely that Merton's sense of the necessity of freedom in prayer has something to do with it. This judgment is based on Merton's distaste for manuals of piety, schemes of instruction on how to pray, which take no account of the individual person and that person's needs and abilities. It is also grounded in his positive affirmation of freedom. Thus, speaking to a group of religious, he says: "We need to be able to move freely with the Spirit in prayer as each situation demands. That is the real secret of the life of prayer, and that is what the life of prayer is for." Later on, speaking to the same group, Merton declares: "As far as prayer is concerned . . . you can do what you like so long as it makes sense, and the one thing to avoid or not to do is to get hung up on any one thing and say, 'This is the only thing, and everybody who doesn't do this is wrong.' All the old ways are good and all the new ways are good. We can't do everything, so you pick the way that is good for you at the time that is good for you."[50]

Whatever Merton's ambivalence about liturgical prayer, such prayer does not exhaust his sense of the corporate dimension of prayer. All prayer, even solitary prayer, has a corporate character. Merton writes: "When I pray I am no longer myself talking to God or myself loved by God. When I pray the Church prays in me. My prayer is the prayer of the Church." This is as true of private prayer as it is of liturgy.

If I am going to pray validly and deeply, it will be with a consciousness of myself, as being more than just myself when I pray. In other words, I am not just an individual with grace when I pray. When I pray I am, in a certain sense, everybody. The mind that prays in me is more than my own mind, and the thoughts that come up in me are more than my own thoughts because this deep consciousness when I pray is a place of encounter between myself and God and between the common love of everybody.[51]

That prayer links us to others is true in a still larger and more inclusive sense. In the process of divinization we come to see God's presence in all creation. Our shared identity with Christ links us with all humanity. This is what it means to be in Christ, to have the form of Christ in the world. Merton writes:

a new kind of relationship is established between our own freedom and that ultimate freedom and spirit: the God who is love and who is also the "Lord of History." At the same time a new relationship with other men comes into being: instead of living for ourselves, we live for them. Ideally speaking, if we all lived in this kind of altruistic concern and engagement, human history would culminate in an epiphany of God in man. Mankind would visibly be "Christ."[52]

It is this further dimension of the corporate nature of prayer which led Merton toward the end of his life to address the problem of the relation of contemplation to action in a fresh way.

CONTEMPLATION AND ACTION

Merton acknowledges that the tension between activism and contemplation is an ancient one in the church. It has become particularly acute in our own day as those both within and outside the church have attacked the role of the contemplative orders or criticized the church for its alliance with the status quo. Merton too is alarmed at the reduction of the Christian life to activism by some, and he deplores the opposition to prayer that he began to find even among the clergy at the very end of his life. In a conference on prayer at Calcutta in the last days of his life he said:

You will not believe me when I tell you some of the things that are being said, of people going to a priest in confession, complaining of their inability to pray. The priest says, "Why pray? I don't pray. Why should you? Prayer is irrelevant. Prayer is medieval. It is immaturity." You will think I am joking. "Your action is your prayer, and if your action is twenty-four hours a day, your prayer is twenty-four hours a day."[53]

One would not expect Merton to be friendly to such views of prayer, but knowing his view of the social character of prayer, neither would one expect him to repudiate activism. Indeed his response is not a counterattack on activisim. He urges a balance between contemplation and action even for monks. On the one hand he insists that the whole church and the

culture profit by having men and women who withdraw from activities in the world and demonstrate "a
certain quality of life, a level of awareness, a depth of
consciousness, an area of transcendence and of adoration which are usually not possible in an active secular
existence."[54] Love alone is enough, says Merton, re-
gardless of whether it produces anything. "It is better,"
he thinks, "for love not to be especially oriented to
results. . . . Love is sufficient unto itself."[55] Yet prayer
has a prophetic character, and contemplatives and
monasteries have a prophetic vocation. Merton's own
later life—his concern and involvement in the areas of
racism, poverty, the Vietnam War, etc.—are illustra-
tions of the depth of his conviction. Merton is also sensitive to the Marxist criticism of religion. Christians
should be able to say with the New Testament that in
the conflict between law and freedom God is on the
side of freedom. Contemplatives, he thought, needed
to prepare themselves to respond to the prophetic aspect of their vocation.[56]

Merton was also responsive to the call for renewal
and change in the church and in the monastic orders.
The foundations of Christian bourgeois society have
been shaken. "That kind of a society no longer exists.
We're living in a world in revolution."[57] Merton calls
for a rethinking and renewal of monastic life, reexamin-
ing the meaning of vocation to contemplation itself,
trying to separate the essentials from the accidentals.
He does not appear to want revolution within the
church or the orders, but he does wish to relax the
rigidities, the legalism, to provide for more individual
differences of pattern of life. He says that in the past the
contemplative life was approached through a process of
detaching the monk from the normal joys of human life
—love, art, music, nature, sports, etc.—for the sake of
the "one thing necessary." Perhaps, he writes, "the one
thing necessary is not that which is left when everything is crossed off, but it is perhaps that which includes

and embraces everything else, that which is arrived at when you've added up everything and gone far beyond."[58] The Christian has to be both separated from the world and also open to it. Though imagination is to play no part in contemplative prayer in the strict sense, since whatever can be "seen" cannot be God, there ought to be a liberation of the imagination and of the senses in meditation and in other dimensions of the contemplative life. The function of image, symbol, music, etc., is to open up the inner self and to incorporate the body and the senses into the total orientation to God.[59] Whether we like it or not we are constantly being bombarded by social images. Rather than suppress the imagination, the contemplative life should liberate and purify it. Imagination can be creative. It can see and discover meanings. The Bible embodies its message in concrete material images, and one must be sensitive to such images in order to receive the divine message.

CHRISTIAN PRAYER AND THE SPIRITUAL DISCIPLINES OF THE EAST

More than any of our writers on prayer, Merton has been interested in the relationship of Christian prayer to the spiritual disciplines used by non-Christians, especially in the East. He wrote extensively on Asian religion and meditational practices and at the very end of his life undertook a journey to the Far East to share in dialogue with monks of other traditions. Since Merton makes an explicit attempt to relate Christian and non-Christian spiritual disciplines, it is important to understand the reasons for his effort.

Certainly a part of the ground of Merton's exploration of the spiritual disciplines of the East is rooted in his own personal history. His early reading of Aldous Huxley's *Ends and Means* (in 1937) played a part in his conversion and introduced him to mysticism. It also—along with his acquaintance (in 1938) with a Hindu monk (Bramachari)—began a process of study and growing openness to the thought and disciplines of the Orient. There are traces of this interest in his writings in the 1950's. The Second Vatican Council in its "Declaration on the Relation of the Church to Non-Christian Religions" supported and confirmed Merton's own views when it recognized the validity of the religious sense of all peoples and races to contemplate the divine mystery and to express it. It also declared that the church rejected nothing which is true and holy in these religions and thereby encouraged the spirit of dialogue. The presence of those experienced in the Eastern spiritual disciplines as visitors at the Abbey of Gethsemani increased his interest. Particularly important were Merton's conversations with the Zen Buddhist D. T. Suzuki. Taken together, these experiences led to a basic attitude which Merton expressed in his comments at the Calcutta meeting in 1968:

I need not add that I think we have now reached a stage of (long-overdue) religious maturity at which it may be possible for someone to remain perfectly faithful to a Christian and Western monastic commitment, and yet to learn in depth from, say, a Buddhist or Hindu discipline and experience.[60]

What this attitude led to in concrete dialogue with the spiritual leaders of India, Tibet, and Thailand is recorded in Merton's posthumously published *Asian Journal.*

Merton was interested in a variety of forms of non-Christian monasticism and mysticism and he studied and wrote about some of the classics of Chinese and Indian religions, but his special interest was in Zen Buddhism. Merton's views of the relationship of Christian and non-Christian prayer and spirituality are most clearly spelled out in his discussions of Zen. Merton did not regard Zen as a religion or theology or even as a mysticism in the religious sense. He saw in Zen a concrete metaphysical intuition. He writes:

Zen is not theology, and it makes no claim to deal with theological truth in any form whatever. Nor is it an abstract metaphysic. It is, so to speak, a concrete and lived ontology which explains itself not in theoretical propositions but in acts emerging out of a certain quality of consciousness and of awareness.[61]

In this sense Zen is compatible with Christianity. Christians as well as Buddhists—and, one might assume, others—can equally well practice Zen. In fact, Merton believes that at the level of psychology and experience there is an analogy, if not an identity, between what is experienced by the Christian mystic and the Zen man. The religious and theological context of Christian belief makes a difference in how the experience is understood. In the Christian context the experience has a special modality; it is inseparable from the mystery of Christ and the collective life of the church. The experience, Merton thinks, must always in some way be "reducible to a theological form that can be shared by the rest of the Church or that shows that it is a sharing of what the rest of the Church experiences."[62]

Nevertheless, it is clear that there *is* much that is shared by all contemplatives. Merton found that he had more in common with some Zen Buddhists than he did with his own "compatriots who were little concerned with religion or only interested in its external practice."[63] Most often Merton is intent on pointing to the similarity at the level of psychology and experience, holding that Zen implies no theology and is in a sense even antitheological. Zen Buddhism denies that words, concepts, symbols can grasp reality or be normative in any way. Nevertheless, one feels in reading Merton that he senses analogies and commonalities at the theological level which he prefers not to explore too fully publicly. Occasionally, in speaking of Suzuki's interpretation of Zen and its parallels in Eckhart, Merton can speak of seeing in Zen a kind of "intuitive affinity for Christian mysticism." He can say that perhaps the "real area for investigation of analogies and correspondences between Christianity and Zen might after all be theology rather than psychology or asceticism." "At least," he writes, "theology is not excluded but it must be a theology as experienced in Christian contemplation, not the speculative theology of textbooks and disputations."[64]

No doubt experience, at least from a Christian point of view, does carry doctrinal implications, and one might wish that Merton had felt freer to pursue his analysis at that level. His chief attention is, however, drawn to the experience itself and to the metaphysical intuition, as he calls it, sought and achieved in Zen disciplines. What is this experience and intuition and what is its significance for Christian contemplative prayer?

Both of the great contemplative traditions (East and West) agree that by spiritual disciplines a person can radically change and attain "a deeper meaning, a more perfect integration, a more complete fulfillment" than is possible in the active life. Both agree that the way is through the renunciation of that "self" which seeks its own aggrandizement and that a certain "purification" of the will and intelligence can open one up to a higher understanding of the meaning of life and of the very nature of Being itself.[65]

The aim of Zen is the direct experiential intuition into reality. What stands in the way is the empirical ego, the sense of self, the forms (words, concepts, symbols, etc.) through which the empirical self attempts to grasp, and thinks itself capable of grasping, its own reality and that of the "external" world. Zen is antidualistic to the point of rejecting even the dualism assumed in the disjunction "form/formlessness." The assertion of formlessness would seem to presuppose its opposite. But since reality is beyond formlessness and form, this assumed disjunction must not stand in the way of that direct awareness which is pure consciousness. Pure consciousness *is* the reality. The Zen experience is the resolution of all oppositions in a pure void. The void is not merely negative. Paradoxically it is experienced as fullness, as Being, as "suchness" or "thusness." So Suzuki can posit the equation "Zero=Infinity and Infinity=Zero." The void, the emptiness that is reached through the negation of all forms, of all oppositions, *is* reality, is fullness. The consciousness is consciousness of *nothing,* and this is pure consciousness. The seeing is seeing *nothing,* and this is pure seeing. Paradoxically, pure seeing is no seeing, for it is beyond subject/object. It is seeing itself. Mind is no mind. It is "minding." Thus Zen is "liberation from all forms of bondage to techniques, to exercises, to systems of thought and of spirituality, to specific forms of individual spiritual achievement, to limited and dogmatic social programs."[66] The further implication is that since this pure consciousness is nowhere and of nothing it can be everywhere and in everything. We do not need to "leave the point where we are and seek it somewhere else." Merton finds Zen illumination analogous to and perhaps identical with the illumination experienced by some Christian mystics. It is like the knowing in the cloud of unknowing, like the *todo y nada* of St. John of the Cross and the emptiness of Eckhart's "Ground" or Boehme's "Ungrund."[67] "The final awakening of the Zen consciousness is not simply the loss of self, but the finding and gift of self in and through all."[68] The language with which Zen speaks of the experience is, says Merton, not metaphysical but poetic and phenomenological. It is to be interpreted in the same way as the figurative terms Western mystics use to describe their experience of God.

It is difficult to be sure whether Merton wants to

assert that behind the poetic, figurative, and phenomenological language the reality is the same, or that the experience is the same but the reality is differently understood or interpreted because the languages are different. In the language of metaphysics we say that the intuition of Being is an intuition of a ground of openness, a kind of ontological openness "which communicates itself to everything that is. . . . Openness is not something to be acquired, but a radical gift."[69] There is a nonmetaphysical way of stating this, Merton says. We need not use the language of immanence and transcendence of God or speak of God as Being. Rather, we can speak of God as Freedom and Love, or as grace and presence. These ways of speaking should not be opposed to each other. They should be regarded as two ways of expressing the same kind of consciousness or as varying ways of approaching it.[70] In discussing D. T. Suzuki, Merton puts it even more strongly:

The greatest religions are all in fact very simple. They all retain very important co-essential differences, no doubt, but in their inner reality Christianity, Buddhism, Islam, and Judaism are extremely simple (though capable, as I say, of baffling luxuriance) and they all end up with the simplest and most baffling thing of all: direct confrontation with Absolute Being, Absolute Love, Absolute Mercy or Absolute Void, by an immediate and fully awakened engagement in the living of everyday life.[71]

The reader of Merton's writings in the last two decades of his life senses a certain dissolving tension. He wishes to preserve the distinctiveness between the Christian Way and other ways for theological or ecclesial reasons, and yet he moves more and more toward relaxing that tension and finds analogy, parallel, even identity beneath historical cultural, linguistic, and other differences. Increasingly his own interpretation of Christianity seems to be influenced by Zen. In part this can be seen in his growing utilization of Eckhart to illustrate the meaning of Christian mysticism. It can be seen also in his reinterpretation of the monastic goal of purity of heart. In earlier interpretations of purity of heart, the heart that is pure is a distinct and separate self-consciousness. Merton sees in the consciousness of Being (whether considered positively or negatively, i.e., apophatically) something that goes beyond reflexive self-awareness. The individual is aware, but the consciousness is a consciousness of himself as "a self to be dissolved in self-giving, in love, in 'letting go,' in ecstasy, in God—there are many ways of phrasing it."[72] A similar kind of openness to reinterpreting traditional patterns of thought and to using alternative conceptual frameworks and languages is present elsewhere. Partly this openness is the result of Merton's growing critical awareness that the modern consciousness is different from that of past periods of religious and theological history, that patterns of thought adequate and acceptable five hundred years ago are completely strange to modern man.[73] Partly it is the result of his awareness of new modes of thought that can be utilized to express and interpret the mystic's experience and that are not limited to the West or to a particular time in history. His references to people like Marcel and Teilhard as well as to psychologists like Fromm make this clear. But even more there is in Merton the continuing awareness of the limitations of all concepts, all language, all systems of thought, all cultural perspectives, to express the inexpressible. And just as God transcends all knowledge and all modes of expression, so too the goal for the individual transcends all cultural forms. Final integration is a state of transcultural maturity in which one "apprehends his life fully and wholly from an inner ground that is at once more universal than the empirical ego and yet entirely his own." He is in a certain sense "cosmic" and "universal man. . . . He is in a certain sense identified with everybody: or, in the familiar language of the New Testament, . . . he is 'all things to all men.' "[74] Thus "the man who has attained final integration is no longer limited by the culture in which he has grown up."[75] It appears to me that it is just Merton's apophatic sense which both leads him to see the limitations of all languages and conceptual systems and allows him the freedom to be open to the varying ways of understanding the reality experienced by the mystic, whatever his culture or religious framework. We wonder and we wish that we could see what developments Merton's thought might have taken had he lived to complete his Asian trip and return to America to continue his writing and pursue the contemplative life. We sense that Merton himself was puzzling over next steps and that he was open to the new. In a paper on the new Christian consciousness, published after his death, he had written:

There must be a better reply to the Cartesians than the mere reaffirmation of the ancient static and classic positions. It is quite possible that the language and metaphysical assumptions of the classic view are out of reach of many modern men. It is quite plausible to assert that the old Hellenic categories are indeed worn out, and that Platonizing thought, even revivified with shots in the arm from Yoga and Zen, will not quite serve in the modern world. What then? Is there some new possibility, some other opening for the Christian consciousness today?[76]

8
Karl Rahner—
Transcendental Thomism

KARL RAHNER (b. 1904) is a Jesuit theologian, now
retired from teaching posts at the Universities of Mu-
nich and Münster. He contributed as much as any other
theologian to the opening up of Catholic thought represented by Vatican Council II. He has been a prolific
author, but his *Foundations of Christian Faith: An Introduction to the Idea of Christianity* presents his basic
approach.

Rahner recognizes that prayer is a problem for contemporaries. The spiritual climate has changed from
an earlier era. We have become spiritually hardened.
"Prayer lives among us as a wraith of what it was."[1]
The difficulties are first of all intellectual. In a time
when the reality of God is questioned, prayer itself
comes into question. Or even if the reality of God be
granted in some sense, it is questioned whether this
reality can be addressed "within a personal relationship as our inner-most, intimate, truest, personally ap-
proachable Thou."[2] Prayer is thought of as a "mythological manifestation of a human reality which
essentially refers to our neighbor."[3] Processes of secularization have been powerful and widespread. Prayer
whose reference point is the transcendent has been
subjected to ideological criticism and reduced to a
projection—an expression of the human fear of existence.[4] Beyond this, petitionary prayer poses a partic-

ular problem. It is regarded by many as a pointless flight from real life tasks. The expectation that God will intervene from outside the world is useless. God, if God does exist, exists "as absent-present at an infinite distance as the bare horizon of all human activity and as one about whom we can at most be silent."[5] The intellectual difficulties that the modern age has with prayer are centered in the difficulties our age has with the problem of God. There is a sense in which Rahner's whole theology is an effort to respond to this problem. In relation to prayer it asks: "Is it possible to pray today?" and "What form must prayer take today if it is to be meaningful?"[6] We will return to these questions and Rahner's answer, showing how Rahner's approach to the theology of prayer is rooted in his basic theological method.

The difficulties with prayer are not simply intellectual. They are also cultural, in the sense that weariness, indifference, routinization, the rush and feverishness of everyday life, make prayer difficult and turn it into a "superficial, mechanical, slipshod lip-service, the performance of an external task to be got through as quickly as possible in order to get back to more pleasant things."[7] Where prayer comes from the real depth of human needs there stands the accusation that God has been deaf to human pleading. "God has not answered. We have cried but there has been no response."[8]

File after file we lay before Him: the unheard prayers of the children dying from starvation and of infants frozen by paralysis; the cries of children beaten to death, of exploited slaves and betrayed women, of those crushed by injustice, liquidated in concentration camps mutilated and dishonoured. Only the silence of God meets those bewildered questions raised to heaven by perplexed minds in every age: Why do the wicked prosper, and the good fail? . . . Why is world history a swirl of stupidity, meanness, and brutality?[9]

THE ROAD TO SELF-SURRENDER

There is for Rahner a level of difficulty in prayer that is deeper than the intellectual problems of the secularized mind, the trivialization of everyday life, the unanswered petitions voiced out of human need. One could call it the existential dimension of the problem of prayer. It is not simply that God does not respond to the particular needs which we bring to him but that he is silent in the face of any and all prayer. "When I pray," writes Rahner, "it's as if my words have disappeared down some deep, dark well, from which no echo ever comes back to reassure me that they have struck the ground of Your heart."[10] It is not just that the particular requests are not granted but that I do not really apprehend God's being there. If God's silence is really a word of promise and one is really in prayer to present one's life, one's own self to God, then this is the biggest difficulty of all. "It is completely beyond my strength," writes Rahner.[11] "If I were just able to give You in prayer the only thing You want: not my thoughts and feelings and resolutions, but myself."[12] Prayer requires self-surrender, and this is its most profound difficulty: "I am a stranger even to myself." "And how can I seek You, O distant God, how can I give myself up to You, when I haven't even been able as yet to find myself?"[13]

This sense of inability, of the "barren wastes of my own emptiness," combined with the silence of God, makes prayer especially difficult.[14] Prayer then becomes a waiting. The waiting is a "silent standing by until You, who are ever present in the inmost center of my being, open the gate to me from within."[15] One does not know when or how this moment may come, whether now, or in the future, or at death. Daily prayer is therefore an "awful waiting," a clearing of the ground so that the soul will be ready for that "precious moment when you will offer it the possibility of losing itself in the finding of You."[16]

For Rahner it is not enough to point to the inability of self-surrender and the consequent waiting upon God. There is still a darker side to this inability. It is loneliness and despair. We are engaged in a flight from ourselves. The world is futile. We recognize that we are shadowed by death. For some this is an awareness of the absolute worthlessness of human existence. Rahner calls this despair "perverted pride."[17]

The recognition of one's nothingness and worthlessness is, however, the road to self-surrender and awareness of God. "It is in the darkness of one's knowledge of complete personal worthlessness that the light of the presence of God begins to dawn."[18] We find God, not despite our nothingness, but *because* of our realization of it. Such language concerning the existential difficulty of prayer discloses much of Rahner's view of the heart of prayer. Rahner writes: "Prayer is that act in which man gives himself wholly to God."[19] It is a "complete silent oblation of self, and an entire surrender to God."[20] It is unconditional surrender. In more technical theological language Rahner writes:

Prayer is an act of the virtue of religion, i.e., an act of an intellectually endowed creature by which the creature turns towards God by acknowledging and praising His limitless superiority explicitly or implicitly and by subjecting itself to that superiority (in faith, hope and charity). Hence, prayer is an act by which (a) man as a whole "actualizes" himself and (b) by which this thus actualized human reality is subjected and, as it were, surrendered to God.[21]

COMPREHENDING THE REALITY OF GOD

Prayer for Rahner is then the act in which one gives oneself wholly to God. It is unconditional surrender. The difficulty is that the reality of God has become

problematic in the contemporary world. A theology of
prayer in the secularized West must recognize this situation for what it is, and must discover a way of making
the reality of God comprehensible. Rahner does not
attempt to do this by appealing to the authority of the
church, to Scripture, or to revelation, for these resources for grounding the awareness of the reality of
God are just the ones which are suspect in the modern
world. Rather, Rahner turns to human experience, and
to the self's experience of self-transcendence in its own
thinking, in its own freedom and responsibility, and to
the self's experience of dependence. These dimensions
of human experiencing are universal, for they are made
possible by the very structure of the self. Though the
awareness of such experience and its meaning may be
suppressed or diminished, the experience is there for
all contemporary men and women. Its reality and
meaning can be evoked in order to open up the question of God for contemporary minds.

There is presupposed in all human knowledge a
structure of the self that makes possible infinite self-
transcendence. The human being has the possibility of
unlimited questioning in relation to any truth, any
known object, even its own self. There is in this knowing process the implicit awareness of an ever-receding
(an infinite) horizon. Man experiences a radical openness which Rahner calls an openness to being. The
being to which we are open in all our experience, implicitly at least, and perhaps consciously at times, is a
mystery. It is not an object and it cannot be objectified.
It is an infinite horizon, unfathomable, limitless. "Mystery" is the transcendence presupposed by man's own
self-transcendence. Experiences of this mystery
Rahner calls "transcendental experiences." The source
of such experience, the reality presupposed in and accompanying every act of self-transcendence, whether
in knowing or in freedom and responsibility, is what
Rahner means by "God."

Insofar as this subjective, non-objective luminosity of the subject in its transcendence is always orientated towards the holy mystery, the knowledge of God is always present unthematically and without name, and not just when we begin to speak of it. All talk about it, which necessarily goes on, always only points to this transcendental experience as such, an experience in which he whom we call "God" encounters man in silence, encounters him as the absolute and the incomprehensible, as the term of his transcendence which cannot really be incorporated into any system of coordinates. When this transcendence is the transcendence of *love*, it also experiences this term as the *holy* mystery.[22]

So too does the human awareness of dependence (not just relative but absolute dependence) point to the mystery of being, which is God.

What we have called the implicit awareness of the mystery of being, of the infinite horizon of all thinking and all freedom and responsibility, Rahner calls the pre-apprehension of being. It is an "unthematic," i.e., unconceptualized, unfocused, unreflective, but ever-present knowledge of the infinity of reality. In transcendental experiences this pre-apprehension may become reflective. When this occurs, man may become consciously aware that "spirit is more than a piece of this temporal world, . . . that the meaning of man is not exhausted in the meaning and happiness of this world, . . . [that] the experience of risk and venturesome trust which has no provable justification deducible from mere worldly success [is worthwhile]." This is the experience of eternity, of God. These are moments when "man's whole existence comes into play, in which man is brought up against his life in its entirety, in which the meaning and fulfillment or failure of that life is weighed in its entirety." Such moments may happen for any of us.

Have we ever been silent although we wished to defend ourselves, although we were treated with less than justice? Did we ever forgive although we got no thanks for it and our silent pardon was taken for granted? Did we once obey not because we had to or would otherwise have suffered unpleasant consequences, but merely because of that mysterious, speechless, incomprehensible force we call God and his will? Have we ever made a sacrifice without thanks, acknowledgement or even sentiments of inner peace? Have we ever been thoroughly lonely? Have we had to take a decision purely on the verdict of our conscience, when we cannot tell anybody or explain to anybody, when we are quite alone and know we are making a decision no one can make for us and for which we shall be responsible to eternity? Have we ever tried to love God when no wave of heartfelt enthusiasm sustains us, when we cannot exchange ourselves and life's pressures with God, when we think we are dying of such love, when it feels like death and absolute negation, when we seem to be summoned into the void and the wholly unheard-of, when everything is apparently becoming incomprehensible and seemingly meaningless? Have we perhaps done our duty when we felt we could do it only with the consuming feeling that we were denying ourselves and blotting ourselves out, when we felt we could do it only by perpetrating a horrible stupidity for which no one would thank us? Were we once good to a person from whom no echo of gratitude and understanding returned, and we were not even rewarded with the conviction of having acted "selflessly," responsibly?[23]

These transcendental experiences in which the whole self is involved reflectively may raise the reality of God to awareness. It is to such experiences that the meaning of the term "God" refers at the level of conscious awareness. Prayer and the God who is addressed in prayer are to be understood within the framework of Rahner's notion of transcendental experience. To those therefore who would find prayer questionable because the reality of God is a problem, Rahner would say that the reality of God is presupposed in the very structures of human self-transcendence and is experienced unthematically in and through all our other experience. The reality of God rises to conscious awareness in experiences in which the wholeness of our existence comes into play. In such experiences the implicit or explicit grounding of a decision or an action transcends the present moment, its meaning and context. Prayer can only be understood in relation to the awareness of this transcendent dimension.

Though prayer can only be understood in relation to human awareness of the transcendent, of the infinite horizon, of the mystery of being, nevertheless the awareness of the reality of God is not enough to make prayer what it is. Prayer involve, addressing God. It involves surrender. It involves submerging ourselves more and more deeply in this mystery in knowledge and freedom. Rahner puts it in these words:

Prayer can be itself only when it is understood as the last moment of speech before the silence, as the act of self-disposal just before the incomprehensibility of God disposes of one, as the reflexion immediately preceding the act of letting oneself fall, after the last of one's own efforts and full of trust, into the infinite Whole which reflexion can never grasp.[24]

Rahner attributes this possibility finally to God. *"God* is the very possibility of address, he himself brings our prayer about when we pray."[25] If this is so, he can also be the one who is addressed. Whether this possibility is related to man's essence, whether it is made possible only through grace, or through the fact that God revealed himself in history in Jesus Christ, Rahner does not at this point attempt to settle. That such a possibility exists is shown by the fact that such prayer exists. The axiom that it is legitimate to argue from reality to possibility applies here. Praying is a historical constant of humanity. Whatever its historical forms, "it always appears as that mysterious procedure by which a person lets himself go into the ultimate mystery of his existence as such, trustingly, explicitly, thematically."[26] We can start from the fact of man praying, as we start from the fact of man thinking or man taking responsibility in his freedom, and we can then discover what it is in man and in reality that makes prayer not only possible but also in some sense necessary.

How Prayer Can Be Conceived as a Dialogue

If Rahner's way of overcoming the threat to belief in
God is successful, what of the second difficulty, the difficulty of understanding God as a person who can address
and be addressed? Rahner approaches this issue in two
ways, by clarifying the notion of "person" in relation to
our understanding of God and by exploring and reinterpreting the notion of prayer as dialogue. The intellectual problem is that what we think of as God's contribution to the dialogue is experienced as our own psychic state or activity.[27] Attempts to resolve the issue
will be unsatisfactory if the relation between man and
God is naively thought to be analogous to an interhuman dialogue. Prayer is thought to be a dialogue because we believe that God says "something" to us in
response to our prayer. Suppose, asks Rahner, that we
were to say that "in prayer we experience ourselves as
the ones spoken by God, as the ones arising from and
decreed by God's sovereign freedom in the concreteness of our existence."[28] Prayer would then be dialogue
because we ourselves are God's saying. God's most original word to us is not some separate momentary word.
God's word is we ourselves as integral total entities. In
prayer we can think of ourselves as "spoken by God."
God's address to us in prayer is our experience of ourselves as arising from and decreed by God's sovereign
freedom in the concreteness of our existence. This is a
unique and incomparable kind of dialogue which cannot be modeled simply on interhuman conversation.
That human analogy is too limited, for God transcends
the categories of the finite world. It is important to
realize that God's part of the dialogue (ourselves as
spoken by God) is always particular, concrete, historical, personally experienced.[29] It is at the same time
transcendental in Rahner's language, which means that

it is a universal human reality, "always and everywhere realized and known in and together with man's spiritual and free self-realization as the unthematic condition of the possibility of all human existence."[30]

The question of the dialogic character of prayer is not, however, simply a question of whether there is some way of retaining the old language for prayer in the contemporary world. The question as to whether God addresses man, whether there is a real partner in dialogue, is finally the question of whether there is one who responds and whether there is any response. Can God conceived as Holy Mystery be said to answer prayer? This issue is seen in one of its critical forms in what Rahner says about secondary causes. He accepts Thomas Aquinas' statement that God acts through secondary causes, but he says that what Thomas meant by this was that God causes the world, not that he causes in any direct way *in* the world. What this means is that God does not intervene in the causal processes that are studied and understood as operative in the object world. It would be wrong from Rahner's point of view for anyone to think that if it rained following a prayer for rain, or if one received a desired object for which one had prayed, that God "caused" the results in the sense that God brought about some changes in the causal processes normally the province of meteorology or psychology or sociology. God does not answer prayer in this way. There is, however, a more subtle metaphysical causality involving the very fact that God is the transcendental ground of the world. Whatever is, cannot be sufficiently understood simply by referring it to the efficient causes operating within the object world. The emergence of the new, of that which is not simply the reorganization of what was initially present, suggests the presence of something "more" than efficient causes.[31] Similarly with objects of our choice: if and when they can be assimilated into our absolute openness to God in unconditional surrender to him and without jeopardizing that openness, and if they can be made part of that unconditional acceptance of God's word (which we ourselves are), they can be regarded as a moment in the dialogue between God and man. Since these objects of our choice do not distort or detract from that fundamental openness, we may call them part of God's address to one of us.[32] They may be thus regarded as expressions of God's will and causality.

Rahner makes much the same point in *Foundations of the Christian Faith* when he discusses whether it is appropriate to represent the emergence of a "good idea" as an inspiration of God. It is clear, he says, that one should trace such a "good idea" back in whatever causal chain may have produced it. God did not produce it or inspire it in the sense of intervening in the psychological processes which brought this "good idea" to birth. However, once "I experience myself as a transcendental subject in my orientation to God and accept it," and the moment "I accept this concrete world in all its concreteness and in spite of all the functional interconnectedness of all its elements" as the concrete world in which my relationship to this ground unfolds historically, then I can say that this "good idea" is willed by God who is its ground.[33] Indeed, everything can be so regarded if I accept, understand, and respond to it in this way. For Rahner such an understanding of the presence of God in acts or events does not deny human freedom.

What Rahner has said about the possibility of conceiving of prayer as a form of dialogue provides the clue for understanding his answer to the question as to whether God may be thought of as a person. Just as the dialogue that is prayer is unique and incomparable, analogous but radically different from interhuman dialogue, so too we may speak of God as personal, though God is not and cannot be a person in the same sense that a human being is a person. Rahner writes: "If anything at all can be predicated of God, then the concept

of 'personhood' has to be predicated of him." We ought
to speak of God's personhood only if and when we
relate that notion to "the ineffable darkness of the holy
mystery."[34]

THE SELF-COMMUNICATION OF GOD

The intellectual difficulties that the modern age has
with the problem of prayer are critical for any contemporary theology of prayer. They have to do with the
contemporary world's questions about the reality of
God and the way in which any viable conception of God
may allow for the kind of dialogical relationship between man and God that has traditionally been the
very presupposition of the act of prayer. There are
many of course who lead a simple and, for Rahner, a
naive (in the good sense) religious life. For them God is
an "immediate really existing obvious reality," whom
we address as Thou, as "Our Father." But there is more
to it than this. God is not just something alongside other
things. God is not any kind of particular being. God is
not a particular concrete Thou. God is the "ultimate,
original, incomprehensible ground" of all things; ineffable, sacred, incomprehensible mystery. God is the silence in which we are silenced.[35] In this sense, as transcendent, God is no-where. But God is gracious. His
personal self-communication is everywhere except
where the "No" of sin, of shutting out God, is spoken.
This means that there is no secular world empty of God,
no place of worship or explicit prayer to which God is
limited. "God is everywhere as the world's grace."
Whenever we reach the ultimate truth of anything, we
have already broken through to God's grace. Thus the
history of the world, of its ideas, of its culture, is really
"just the history of this gracious self-communication of
the absolute and transcendent God."[36] This history,
which Rahner calls the body and history of God, in-

cludes definite events in which the divine life at the roots of all reality comes to light, is manifested, and takes visible shape in the word, in sacrament, in worship.

The coming to light of the divine life in the world and in history centrally occurred in Jesus Christ, in his cross and resurrection. It came to light in such a way that it became evident that this self-communication of God is irrevocable, and in this sense eschatological. It has become manifest that this self-communication is "without repentance, that it prevails, is victorious, and will be victorious," that it has already "saved the world in its innermost reality and brought it salvation."[37]

The self-communication of God in the historical Jesus and the consequent possibility of the Christian's union with Christ and participation in his life and death makes possible the Christian's courage to address God, even in a world that talks of the death or absence of God. Because of Christ we no longer look on God as the Almighty Judge. We know of his love for men. Through Christ we find a new dignity. We find the strength to pray, realizing that we do not pray alone, but through him. He has taught us how to pray by means of the Lord's Prayer, and by modeling in his own life both our humanness in our desire for self-preservation and the possibility of utter self-surrender and submission to God's will.

Such prayer is made possible by the Holy Spirit. As Augustine said, there is a basic restlessness and discontent in human nature. There is a craving for the divine. Our hearts are restless, and the possibility that this restlessness can be allayed lies in the presence of the Holy Spirit within us. We choke off this craving for the divine with our sin and worldliness. Man is neither self-sufficient nor rational, but God dwells below our apparent rationality and the darker irrational side of human nature disclosed by depth psychology. The spirit of God dwells with us as our true infinity: "The mind of man is not consciousness alone. . . . Below the level of consciousness are infinite possibilities, unfathomed depths, unmeasured horizons." The depths are not "pools of stagnant bitterness" but "the waters of infinity springing up into eternal life."[38] Behind and through the dark forces, faith can see the power and presence of the Holy Spirit. But we must invite the Spirit to speak, and the presence of the Spirit of God within us is the source of our prayers. He is working on us, in us, and for us especially in "that most important of all our activities—prayer."[39]

Thus we pray not only with the human in us but with the divine. The Spirit of God prays in us. This is what gives dignity to our prayer. It is this Spirit which is active in us even when we know not what to pray, or when we pray in a time of spiritual dryness. The "unfailing power of our prayer is the Spirit of God praying within us."[40]

Rahner is as conscious of the *problem* of prayer as any of our authors. In part his theological interpretation of prayer addresses the issue of the possibility of prayer in a secular age that has difficulty with the very notion of God. This is the particular significance of his attempt to show that there is an unthematic awareness of the presence of God, understood as mystery—infinite, unfathomable, universally accessible—in all human experiencing. Against this background understanding he goes farther, showing how this universal self-communication of God gets particularized in the historical Jesus and in the history of the Christological reality in the ongoing life of the Christian community. What was and is implicit in all human experience has become explicit through Christ's revelation of the meaning of God's self-communication for human existence. This particularization and historicization of God's self-communication leads to a distinctively Christian understanding of prayer. Within that understanding many distinctions need to be made, both qualitatively in relation to value and descriptively in relation to types of prayer. In addition, the specific question about the possibility of petitionary prayer can be addressed in a distinctively Christian way. To these aspects of Rahner's theology of prayer we now turn.

QUALITATIVE DIFFERENCES IN PRAYER

Prayer, according to Rahner, is not all on the same level. Qualitatively prayer varies according to the degree and kind of self-surrender which it expresses, since the heart of prayer is unconditional self-surrender. Even routine prayer, where there is little or no real devotion, is not without value, for it gives objective glory to God and may be a preparation for a more existential self-surrender. The value of the prayer depends on the degree or intensity of the human self-surrender. God's grace allows this differentiation according to the greater or lesser actualization of the person.[41] Just as intensity of self-surrender is one mark of value and differentiation in prayer, so too the dignity and efficacy of prayer reflect the degree to which the person praying is aroused and animated by grace. The dignity of *Christian* prayer is distinctive in that it is the prayer of one who has been elevated to the supernatural order and has been divinized by *sanctifying* grace.[42] So Rahner can say that the prayer of the justified is of a different order than the prayer of the sinner. It follows too that since grace can increase, and sanctifying grace can itself be brought about by prayer, the dignity, merit, and power of prayer can increase.

These distinctions with respect to the quality and value of prayer would *seem* to imply that non-Christian prayer, or even non-Catholic prayer, is somehow inferior, since Rahner holds that man's divinization by the created and uncreated grace of Christ is a sharing in the divine nature, and that a union with Christ includes union with the mystical body of Christ which is the church. What does Rahner believe about the prayer of pagans and non-Catholic Christians?

Clearly Rahner does not believe that God has limited access to himself only to those who are faithful Christians, let alone Catholic Christians. Nor does he believe that Christians or Catholic Christians are the only human beings who are "justified" in the theological sense. He believes that there is a supernatural existential element in every man which underlies and makes possible every act and decision of man and all human knowing. Therefore grace is always present "for every man as *a priori* transcendental consciousness and as an offer made by God."[43] If the offer of grace present in the supernatural existential is accepted, if justification takes place, it takes place in and through the power Christians know in Christ, whether or not those who have accepted the offer have responded explicitly to the historical Christ. Such persons, if justified, "belong in some true sense to the Church."[44] It is not enough, says Rahner, to consider only the social and external structure of the church and to leave out of account its generation by the Holy Spirit. The prayer of justified non-Catholics possesses "the same dignity and the same value as the prayer of those who are members in the strict sense."[45] Such prayer bears witness in some way to the Catholic Church. Rahner believes, of course, that visible church membership has a positive influence on the value of prayer.

Not everything that looks like prayer is genuine prayer, for the heart of prayer is self-surrender. Conversely where there is real self-surrender, there is prayer in some real sense. Rahner calls such prayer "virtual prayer." Self-denial includes self-surrender and therefore it is prayer. If it includes explicit reference to God, Rahner is willing to call it formal prayer. He writes: "Every express reference of the course of our lives to God in faith, hope, and love, which is formally giving honour to God, is also by that very fact formal prayer."[46] So love of neighbor and commitment of one's life to others, which may be easier for contemporary men and women than expressly "religious" acts, are a kind of "opening onto formal prayer," and if they include explicit reference to God, they become formal prayer in Rahner's sense.

LITURGICAL AND NONLITURGICAL PRAYER

One question that is often critical for Catholic Christians centers on the relationship between private prayer and communal prayer, or between liturgical prayer in the technical sense and nonliturgical prayer, either private or communal. As we saw in considering Merton's understanding of prayer, this was an issue which created some tension in his life and thought. Rahner discusses this issue when he treats prayer as an act of the church. For Rahner the distinction between communal and individual prayer is a false one, or at least a secondary one. Christians are always Christians in the community of Christ. Individual prayer can never be that of an isolated individualist. It flows into the community, into its worship and its actualization as community. It can do this because for Rahner there is an invisible unity of all of the faithful, as well as the external visible social unity of the church. The reverse is also true with respect to the communal prayer of the faithful. Every individual depends on everyone else in his or her prayer. Though this is true of every prayer, it is particularly manifest in communal prayer. Because we are members of one body, "everyone ought to pray for everyone else."[47]

Technically, only the communal worship explicitly ordered and juridically regulated by the highest authority is called Liturgy. It is obviously an act of the church. For Rahner, however, all acts of Christians performed in the state of grace are true acts of the Mystical Body. Grace always has an ecclesiological character. In this sense there are no such acts which are simply private or individual; and every supernatural prayer, whether apparently private or communal in the non-liturgical sense, can rightly be called an act of the church. What ultimately gives prayer its dignity is the Holy Spirit, and the gift of that Spirit is limited to no one form of prayer, but is present in every form of genuine prayer. While prayer ordered by ecclesiastical authority may have certain advantages, it is not the only prayer which is truly an act of the church, nor is prayer to be distinguished in its value and effectiveness except by reference to the action of the Holy Spirit in it. The Spirit's activity cannot be limited by form or authority. The whole liturgy belongs to the dimension of "sign," and what is signified belongs to another dimension. God's self-communication may occur at points in life "more radically, more definitively, more victoriously, more eschatologically than it does in the sacrament and the liturgical cult."[48] When under God's control a person gives up his whole nature to God or enters into a radically unselfish encounter with his neighbor under certain circumstances, this *is* the authentic reality communicated through the sacrament. In this sense the whole of life is sacred liturgy, and what we designate as worship, as truly liturgy, is "the manifestation, the explicit and intimate form of that hidden mysterious liturgy which we must celebrate in the apparent secularity of life."[49]

PETITIONARY PRAYER

There are distinctions other than those between formal and virtual prayer or between private and communal prayer which can be made in considering the various forms prayer can take. Rahner speaks of many of these in his small book *Happiness Through Prayer*, where he writes of prayers of love, of everyday life, of dedication, of forgiveness, of decision, and of petition. It is petitionary prayer which is something of a testing point for modern interpretations of prayer. Rahner recognizes that the prayer of petition is a special stumbling block for the contemporary world. To many it seems to be either useless or a fraud, or it is spiritualized so that one can only pray for purity of heart, patience, or endurance of our trials and tribulations. Rahner recognizes all this, but he warns us not to be too hasty in sublimating or "demythologizing" petitionary prayer. In the first place, petitionary prayer has always been an important part of the universal history of human prayer and there is a deep need in all of us to turn to God to bring before him our specific and concrete needs. In the second place, many of the difficulties are not new. They have been dealt with already in traditional theology. Rahner says that his own aim is not to answer the skeptical attack on petitionary prayer. Rather, "we seek only such light and strength as will enable us to persevere in prayer."[50] He deals with the problem of petitionary prayer at two levels. On the one hand he observes that our purpose in life is not the pursuit of happiness on earth. We should not complain if God does not give to our prayers the answer demanded by our persistent selfishness. More essentially, the answer to complaints about the inefficacy of prayers of petition has been given to us by God himself in the cross. Christ too knew the desolation of Godforsakenness and has provided the model for our prayer. This model is a mysterious fusion of the will of man and the will of God. The human side is the "cry of elementary self-preservation." The divine side is the subordination of this instinctive will to self-preservation, "wholly and unconditionally to the Will of God." Rahner writes: "Our prayer of petition is, in the ultimate analysis, not a plea for life and the things of this life, but a submission

to the Will of God even when that will points to depri-
vation and perhaps to death."[51] "These two aspects—
man's freedom to plead: man's submission to the free
decision of God—are always found together in true
prayer."[52] Such a defense of prayer will be understood
by the one who prays, for it can be reached only in the
act of praying.

Rahner has more to say about petitionary prayer, and
this is really a development of the notion of submission
to the will of God, but it has a more constructive thrust.
Since the heart of real prayer is self-surrender, there is
no real prayer which is not implicitly grounded in "Thy
will be done." "One cannot come to God in prayer
without giving him oneself, one's whole existence, in
trustful submission and love and in acceptance of the
incomprehensible God who is beyond our understanding not only in his essence but also in his free relationship to us and must be accepted as such."[53] But the
person who brings himself before God in this way is a
concrete person, a "person of daily, profane and banal
needs and anxieties." He must, says Rahner, "place
himself before God in prayer just as he is, just as he may
permissibly know himself to be: willed by God, in the
pressures and needs of his life, which cannot be adequately illumined or simply sublimated into the religious."[54] These needs may be relativized by the act of
prayer, but they are not brushed aside as of no account.
It is petitionary prayer which brings needy man at his
most concrete before God. "It is the form of prayer at
which man is mindful not only of who *God* is, but also
of who *he himself* is."[55] When we understand petitionary prayer in this way the question of how it is granted,
if it is granted, is of secondary importance. Yet there is
doubtless a sense in which it may be possible to say that
a prayer of petition has been granted. We have already
suggested Rahner's view in summarizing what he had
to say about prayer as dialogue.

The Faith of the Individual and the Faith of the Church

Rahner is chiefly concerned with the theological issues relating to prayer. He has relatively little to say about the practice of prayer, though much of his popular writing has a meditative character. He is nevertheless concerned with certain practical issues related to prayer in the life of the church. For example, certain of his writings on prayer are specifically addressed to those in religious orders or to persons responsible for the training and guidance of those in orders. Rahner points out that these remarks have general relevance. One of the critical issues for those in religious orders is the tension between the faith of the individual and that of the church. That this tension is not limited to those in the religious orders is common knowledge. Rahner's response to this problem is to recognize that faith undergoes development, that conceptual articulation and existential appropriation change in relation to the collective faith of the church, which itself undergoes development. It is sufficient for a person, Rahner believes, for entry into a religious order or even for ordination to the priesthood, "that the unsearchable mystery which we call God is present and active in his life and is imparted to us as our goal; he must also be convinced that (a) this intimacy of God with us is indissolubly associated with and arises from a personal relationship to Jesus who died and who was saved completely by the Father in his resurrection, and that (b) the necessary social milieu of faith takes concrete shape in the real Church."[56] Such faith is sufficient as long as the person does not explicitly and firmly reject a church dogma. Rahner expects that such voluntary open-mindedness toward further development will in fact lead to an enlargement and deepening of faith, and that "a faith which is honest about its subjective insecurity is more secure than one which basks in an enforced, self-satisfied subjective security."[57]

What is true for faith is also true for prayer. There must be a relaxation of the rigidity and the regulation of the prayer of the individual. Rahner commends to contemporaries St. Ignatius' practice of leaving the regulation of private prayer simply to the individual's goal. He appears to wish to loosen up the older style of devotion, suggesting that in the past many psychological and psychohygienic functions and exercises were part of private prayer. Now perhaps, he suggests, these can be carried on and even institutionalized in other ways. He comments further that they need to be developed in the light of a far deeper knowledge of modern psychology than was usual in the past.

Rahner calls for "education for prayer." Education for prayer means doctrinal instruction and theological interpretation, but even more it means an experiential grounding of the person. Prayer should not be recommended as "something that is self-evident," but should be related to the "personal experience of an enduring, if mostly anonymous, transcendence of human existence in its wholeness (as a radical unity of grace and nature) reaching into that mystery which we call God and whose reality cannot be merely indoctrinated from outside, but is always experienced by us in our present life, mysteriously, implicitly, and silently."[58]

Experiential education for prayer should also involve a consideration of the situations and experiences (both secular and religious) that can lead to personal prayer, prayer that is more than an externally prescribed duty. Such experiences leading to prayer permeate our whole life. Rahner gives examples: premonition of death, unconditional love of neighbor that does not bring an equally unconditional response, the absolute responsibility for a personal decision, the impenetrability of one's own existence. Such experiences, if they are not repressed, are the very threshold of prayer. The whole of life and explicit prayer can here mutually interpenetrate. Finally, the experiential grounding of prayer must include a Christological dimension, for it is only in relation to Jesus Christ that we draw the courage to address God in a secularized and godless world. It is not easy to acquire such an existential grounding in the ordinary practice of religion. Rahner believes that the direction is given in Matthew 25. What is done to our neighbor *really* happens to Christ, and is not simply *interpreted* as happening to Christ.

NIGHT PRAYER AND THE KINGDOM OF IMAGES

Rahner, as we have said, does not devote much attention in his writing to the actual practice of prayer. There is, however, one striking exception. In one of his most interesting and theologically suggestive papers on prayer, entitled "Spiritual Dialogue at Evening: On Sleep, Prayer, and Other Subjects," Rahner addresses the relationship of prayer to sleep. Purporting to be a conversation between a doctor and a priest, the dialogue has to do with what happens to the human spirit during sleep and how prayer is to be related to this. If we may take Rahner's views to be represented by the priest, it is clear that he sees that something happens during sleep which may alter the spirit and affect our personal waking, thinking, and acting in an uncontrollable way. We may wake up finding our dispositions, our thoughts changed. Is it not possible, he asks, "that practically everything in our lives depends on almost imperceptible alterations in the presuppositions of our actions, imperceptible alterations of mood, of involuntary sequences of thought and so on?"[59] "Something" to which we surrender ourselves in sleep brings this about. And he asks: Is this "something" to which we

surrender ourselves necessarily and in all respects trust-
worthy?

Rahner's answer to his own question is a warning.
The "something" may be dangerous. The old theologians who talked about the demonic spirits and saw
their connection to the "sensitive" part, or as we would
say today, to the subconscious life rooted in the cor-
poreal, were aware of this danger. There are demonic
powers working upon the depths of the unconscious
which make sleep dangerous. The doctor asks if this
means that men should go back to the practice of night
vigils, and Rahner has the priest answer rather that
what all this means is "that before sleep one should
pray, one ought to pray really well."[60]

To this conclusion the doctor responds that the priest
is really calling for a kind of theological night hygiene
of the spirit. The priest replies *no*. What is called for is
real prayer, in which there is unconditional commitment of the whole man. Only then, when such prayer
is real prayer, can it fulfill the other function. Like
every other prayer, night prayer must be seen as "a
surrender of the person to God, as an act of trust in the
outgoing goodness of God, as a willing submission of all
the experiences of the day to the 'order of eternity.' "[61]
But more than this, night prayer must be adapted to
"the peculiar character of that 'kingdom' into which
man in sleep finds his way, so that he 'arms' himself
against the dangers of this region of life in sleep, in a
sense exorcises and blesses it."[62]

But what is the character of this night kingdom?
What are its structural laws to which the demonic influences are themselves subject? Rahner's answer is that
this is the kingdom of the image. As psychic and inten-
tional it has an objective correlative, and as psychoso-
matic it has a concrete correlative—in a word, an
image. This kingdom of images is not unified. The images are mixed, for they originate in both the good and

the evil powers of the spirits. It is the kingdom where both the eternal Logos became flesh and in which the Prince of this World tries to dominate. Rahner writes:

What "moves" the soul in sleep—the soul become defence-less and open—even where there is no dream evidently to hand, are these "images" which are formed there and so supply its guiding images to the personal consciousness throughout the day as well.[63]

Referring to the Jungian theory of archetypes and the collective unconscious, Rahner declares that whatever the truth of the various interpretations of Jung's thought, "it remains true that the spirit of man draws its life also from this kingdom. And above all in sleep. And this because it is formed by these images."[64]

Images are important in and for the praying man. One should bring with him to his sleep good, genuine, holy images. One's power of imagination should be formed by the true archetypes of reality. If one sinks into sleep with such images, "doubtless there will come to meet and greet him out of the kingdom of sleep" similar images. The images of his own prayer will be a kind of principle of selection determining what will be allowed to pass "from the depths of the soul into the soul which is left open." This is possible, says Rahner, because these Christian archetypes are really con-cealed in the depths, because there is no soul that is purely natural, i.e., apart from God (another form of Rahner's teaching on the supernatural existential). For Rahner, what Kant would call "the schemata of the power of imagination" are not neutral and harmless images like space and time; they are either Christian or demonic. "Which of the two sets of images—which con-stitute reality—will in effect become efficacious in us depends too upon which the personal spirit in his wak-ing state has chosen as his."[65] It is for this reason that we need not, and one would think must not, try "to become mystically formless to seize hold of God, since

God has eternally assumed the form, the schema of man." We should attempt in our night prayer in quiet recollection to gather those "great images in which the supreme reality, that of God, has come near to us and impressed itself on this whole world."[66] Even our fantasy has been consecrated down to the deepest roots of man since the Word became flesh. The image in such prayer is a kind of quasi-sacramental sign. In commending this kind of imaginative prayer, Rahner says he is not limiting the imaging to what comes through sight. It should include everything that belongs to the realm of sensibility.

It might be thought that for many this imaging will have a kind of unreality, that it will be mere thought. Rahner replies that an image, or a thought, or a love, or some other act of the spirit, is "more real, more enduring, of greater consequence, of greater validity" than so-called material objects.[67] Imagination is not "mere imagination." What is imagined is really there. It does not exist in time and space so that it could be investigated by the sciences. It transcends time and space, and we can imagine it because "long before we created an image of it this reality caught hold of us and made us very really into its own image and likeness."[68] This is not mere imagination, but a re-presentation of what is truly present, "a mode by which the real is admitted into the sphere of consciousness." These primordial *a priori* images may not be finished and well defined, present in the deeper soul like pictures in an album. Yet, the schemata of the power of the imagination have an *a priori* physiognomy already determined. The actual primordial images are externalized and expressed under the stimulus of the material of experience.[69] Rahner calls attention to the fact that St. Ignatius in his *Spiritual Exercises* places the imaginative way of meditation in the evening so that the image which is to be taken with one to sleep will spring before the mind immediately in the morning.

A New Theology of Prayer

Rahner has called for an experiential education in prayer, and what he has written in his dialogue on sleep could be related to such education in prayer. It is more than this, however. It is part of a new theology of prayer, and Rahner believes that such a theology is vitally important. When men and women are no longer immersed in a religious culture that surrounds them with the evidence of the possibility and the meaning of prayer, much of what formerly came under the heading of mystical prayer, such as teaching about the discernment of the spirits, the night of the senses and of the spirit, etc., must now be carried on by means of a theology that is intelligible to the modern world. Such a theology must be aware of the difficulties contemporary men and women have in praying, and of the special difficulty they have with prayers of petition and prayers that invoke the saints, both of which are regarded by many as purely mythological relics of earlier times.

Rahner has struggled with these critical issues. His effort to define prayer as self-surrender, which both expands and restricts the meaning of prayer, his view of virtual prayer, his discussion of the relation of the prayers of non-Christians and non-Catholics to the prayer of Catholic Christians, are all part of his major effort to expand the horizon of traditional Catholic thought on prayer. Rahner has also placed great emphasis on the existential character of prayer in relation to the boundary situations faced by all human beings. He has placed prayer at the very heart of Christian life. Most important of all, Rahner has addressed the central problem that underlies the erosion of prayer in contemporary life, the problem of God. Whether he has been successful will be a matter for each reader to judge, but he has tried to ground his approach in experience which, since it is universal, is subject to critical reflection by each of us.

9
Abraham J. Heschel—
Prophetic Mysticism

ABRAHAM J. HESCHEL (1907–1972), longtime professor of ethics and Jewish mysticism at the Jewish Theological Seminary, was deeply influenced by his own Hasidic roots. In the later years of his career he was the single most active Jewish thinker related to such causes as the civil rights movement and the debate over the Vietnam War. He was a philosopher, a theologian, and a biblical scholar. Central works are *God in Search of Man* and *The Prophets.*

No contemporary theologian has given prayer a more central place in theology or in the religious life than Abraham Heschel.[1] Prayer is an act of supreme importance. Of all the sacred acts, prayer comes first. Prayer is the essence of spiritual living. Prayer is the quintessence of life. Prayer is the link between the self and God and between the self and the world. It is the means of the transformation and the transcendence of the self. Prayer is the queen of the commandments. No religious act is performed in which prayer is not present. Prayer is an ontological necessity. Prayer defines the very essence of what it means to become a human being. He who has never prayed is not fully human. If we would understand what it means to be human, we must understand what prayer is. But prayer is even more the key to understanding the reality of God. Heschel says again and again: "The issue of prayer is not prayer; the issue of prayer is God."[2]

THE NECESSITY OF PRAYER

The problem of prayer in contemporary life also reflects the human condition in our time and the critical state of the individual and of society's relation to God. For Heschel can attribute the misery and wretchedness pervasive in the human scene to the misunderstanding and neglect of prayer. He can see in the revival and renaissance of prayer the one hope for religious institutions and the human community. Heschel's diagnosis of the human situation is grim:

Emblazoned over the gates of the world in which we live is the escutcheon of the demons. The mark of Cain in the face of man has come to overshadow the likeness of God. There has never been so much guilt and distress, agony and terror. At no time has the earth been so soaked with blood.[3]

Like an Old Testament prophet, Heschel speaks of the world being in flames, consumed by evil. Addressing a conference on aging, Heschel declares:

I see the sick and the despised, the defeated and the bitter, the rejected and the lonely. I see them clustered together and alone, clinging to a hope for somebody's affection that does not come to pass. I hear them pray for the release that comes with death. I see them deprived and forgotten, masters yesterday, outcasts today.[4]

Speaking on religion and race, Heschel says of the plight of the blacks in our society:

My heart is sick when I think of the anguish and the sighs, of the quiet tears shed in the nights in the overcrowded dwellings in the slums of our great cities, of the pangs of despair, of the cry of humiliation which is running over.[5]

Addressing a conference on youth, Heschel says that the problem of our youth is not youth:

The problem is the spirit of our age: denial of transcendence, the vapidity of values, emptiness in the heart. . . . Eclipse of sensitivity is the mark of our age. Callousness expands at the rate of nuclear energy, while moral sensitivity subsides.[6]

For Heschel, it would not be too strong a statement to say that this grim human situation is what it is because human beings do not really pray. They do not pray as they should because they have lost their sense of wonder, their sense of mystery, and the memory which is the source of faith for both the individual and the community. Religion as Heschel understands it begins with wonder, with what he calls radical amazement. The great enemy of spirit and the root of sin is indifference to the sublime wonder of living, taking things for granted. Objectively what corresponds to wonder is mystery. Mystery is a dimension of all existence. It is an ontological category. Being as being is essential mystery. We cannot comprehend why or wherefore being is. "The world," says Heschel, "is something we *apprehend but cannot comprehend.*"[7] Wonder and mystery lead us to God. "God is a mystery, but the mystery is not God."[8] The religious question is what to do with the feeling of mystery and wonder. In this sense religion "begins with a consciousness that something is asked of us."[9]

MEMORY, THE SOURCE OF FAITH

There is a move beyond wonder and the presence of mystery that leads to faith in God and hence to prayer. There is meaning beyond mystery. For us this meaning comes through memory, the memory which is the Bible, the memory of a people, as well as the memory of the individual. The memory is the memory of God's presence in his glory (Shekinah) which is revealed at moments:

The glory is the presence, not the essence of God; an act rather than a quality; a process not a substance. Mainly the glory manifests itself as a power overwhelming the world. Demanding homage, it is a power that descends to guide, to remind. The glory reflects the abundance of good and truth, the power that acts in nature and history.[10]

What is decisive is the awareness of being known, being called to respond to this glory. To believe is to remember. Neither an individual man nor a generation of men can of their own power erect a bridge that leads to God. Faith is the achievement of ages. It is an effort accumulated through the centuries. Memory then is the source of faith, but it is the memory of the community through time. "To have faith is to remember. Jewish faith is a recollection of that which happened to Israel in the past. . . . Recollection is a holy act: we sanctify the present by remembering the past."[11] Yet for Heschel faith is not simply tradition, or recollection. Each of us adds something. Heschel thinks that each of us sometime has experienced the momentous reality of God. The remembrance of that experience and the loyalty to that event is what sustains our faith. Heschel can say of prayer: "Prayer revives and keeps alive the rare greatness of some past experience in which things glowed with meaning and blessing."[12] For Jews, in any case, tradition is not for tradition's sake, but for the sake of survival, of life itself.

The vertical unity of Israel is essential to the horizontal unity of kelal Israel (the community of Israel). Identification with what is undying in Israel, the appreciation of what was supremely significant throughout the ages, the endeavor to integrate the abiding teachings and aspirations of the past into our own thinking will enable us to be creative, to respond, not to imitate or to repeat.[13]

We cannot then of our own power build the bridge to the realm of holiness. Memory is important, critical for the life of faith and for prayer. It is through memory that we know what God would have his relationship to human existence be.

There is a hierarchy of moments for Judaism. God is not equidistant from all ages: "Man may pray to God equally at all places, but God does not speak to man equally at all times. Sinai does not happen every day, and prophecy is not a perpetual process."[14] The importance of memory for Heschel is underscored in the answer he gave to one of his former students who had asked how the spirit attained during the morning services could be preserved through the mundane experiences of the day. Heschel replied: *"Remember* that you prayed."[15]

Faith and prayer depend ultimately upon God, upon the wonder, the radical amazement, the mystery, and the meaning that transcends mystery disclosed in God's Shekinah, and kept vital in living memory. Men and women may be born human beings, but they become *human,* i.e., they express what it is to be essentially human, in prayer. It is prayer which expresses the fact that they are the true partners of God. They are partners of a God who cares and—because he cares— judges, commands, loves, shows mercy. Because they see themselves as partners of God, those who pray strive to embody his will in their actions. The heart of prayer is response to God. It is answer, not request. It is the way in which human beings can testify to his presence. It is a way of keeping open to his presence.

THE GOD WHO CARES

For Heschel, it is God's search for man which is ground for man's search for God. "Religion consists of God's question and man's answer."[16] God searches for man because God does not wish to be alone.

God means: No one is ever alone; the essence of the temporal is the eternal. . . . God means: Togetherness of all beings in holy otherness.[17]

The human meaning of this divine search for man is care, love, compassion.

The puzzle is that men and women do not answer the divine search. They do not respond to the divine question. They ignore God or deny God. They hide from God, though the appearance is that God hides himself.

God is in exile, but *we* have exiled him. "When the doors of this world have been slammed on Him, His truth betrayed, His will defied, He withdraws leaving man to himself. God did not depart of His own volition; He was expelled."[18] God is not at home in this corrupt world, but the universe would be an inferno if it were not that God cares. If it were not for the certainty that God listens to our cry, who could stand the misery and the callousness of our world? For all its cities and its stars the world is dark. Only God hears. Life is possible only because we can know through the biblical tradition that God cares, that he is immediately and directly concerned.

Heschel's view is that the Bible reveals a God who is radically different from that envisaged by the Greek tradition. One of his interpreters writes that for Heschel, God is not the unmoved mover but "the most Moved Mover."[19] Pathos is the central category for the prophetic understanding of God, according to Heschel. Man's deeds move God, affect him, grieve him, or gladden and please him. Pathos characterizes God's relation to the human, not what God is in himself. It is because God reveals himself in his divine pathos that prayer is the central religious act. Prayer can make a difference. Prayer affects God. The true motive of prayer is the human sense of not being at home in the universe and the awareness that God is not at home. "To pray means to bring God back into the world, to establish His kingship for a second at least. To pray means to expand His presence. . . . His being immanent in the world depends on us."[20]

The source of prayer is not feeling but insight—insight into who God is and how he is related to the human world. Prayer is the means by which the gap between God and the human world is overcome. If we do not pray, this gap widens into an abyss. Prayer opens the door to God. It is an invitation to God to "intervene in our lives, to let His will prevail in our affairs."[21] To pray means to overcome distance, to shatter screens, to heal the break between the world and God.

From what we have said it should be clear that for Heschel the heart of prayer is not petition, not human desires or hopes, but God himself. The issue in prayer, says Heschel, is not prayer; the issue is God. Unless there is a concerned God, a God who can be reached in prayer, one will not pray. The meaning of prayer is in the new or renewed relationship to such a God and in the transformation of self and world which the new form of relationship between God and the one who prays makes possible. Therefore Heschel can say that the "purpose of prayer is to be brought to His attention, to be listened to, to be understood by Him, not to know Him, but *to be known to* Him."[22] To be known by him means also to be judged by him, to seek to relate his will to one's life and to society.

Prayer is a confrontation with Him who demands justice and compassion, with Him who despises flattery and abhors iniquity. Prayer calls for self-reflection, for contrition and repentance, examining and readjusting deeds and motivations, for recanting the ugly compulsions we follow, the tyranny of acquisitiveness, hatred, envy, resentment.[23]

In prayer God reaches us as a claim on our being and our action. It is in some such sense that we can understand Heschel's reiterated statement that "we pray in order to pray."[24] Ultimately prayer is not for something other than itself, i.e., other than the new relationship to God (which it is) and by implication what that new relationship makes possible. So too we must understand Heschel's statement "I pray because I am unable to pray."[25]

Prayer can embody a new or renewed relationship. God's silence is not forever. Though we build a wall between ourselves and God, prayer may succeed in penetrating the wall. Even when we seem not to know how to pray, or what to pray, or to have awakened to our need to pray, this condition itself may serve to open the door to God and be accepted as constituting a relationship to him. Heschel writes:

And suddenly I am forced to do what I seem unable to do. Even callousness to the mystery is not immortal. There are moments when the clamor of all sirens dies, presumption is depleted and even the bricks in the walls are waiting for a song. The door is closed, the key is lost. Yet a new sadness of my soul is about to open the door.[26]

When converted to prayer, even our anguish over truth can evoke the dawn of God. Because God is merciful and the possibility of prayer is his gift, our prayer for the ability to pray, even though tainted with vanity and marked by feebleness and ignorance, will be accepted and redeemed by his mercy. God hears not only prayer but the very desire to pray. For those who search for faith, who yearn and fail, Heschel says, "we did not presume to judge."

Let them pray to be able to pray, and if they do not succeed, if they have no tears to shed, let them yearn for tears, let them try to discover their heart and let them take strength from the certainty that this too is a high form of prayer.[27]

Though Heschel points to God's willingness to hear our most immature and struggling efforts, he clearly believes that there is much that can be done to deepen the understanding and practice of prayer. Our troubles with prayer are no doubt related to the secularization of our culture, to the loss of faith in God, etc. They are also related to lack of understanding and lack of training in prayer itself. Prayer has become a forgotten language. We do not refuse to pray; we feel that our tongues are tied and our minds are inert. Therefore we abstain from prayer. Or in public worship we are provided prayer by proxy. The rabbi or the cantor does the praying for the congregation, while the congregation contains men who would not admit that they took prayer seriously. They would think themselves sanctimonious or hypocritical if they prayed. They are "too

sophisticated" to pray. There are of course also psychological and sociological understandings of prayer which
make it difficult for those who accept them to engage
in prayer. Heschel calls for the training of religious
leaders and lay people in the understanding and practice of prayer. His own speaking and writing can be
seen as part of that process of education. To his more
detailed analysis of the act of prayer we now turn.

BECOMING THE OBJECT OF GOD'S THOUGHT

If prayer is fundamentally a response to God's prior
action, how does the human action respond? Heschel
says the beginning of prayer is praise. "To praise is to
make Him present to our minds, to our hearts, to vivify
the understanding that beyond all questions, protests,
and pain at God's dreadful silence is His mercy and
humility."[28] To praise is to bring to awareness the
promise and presence of the divine. Prayer is also the
moment when humility becomes real. Humility is not
a virtue. It is the recognition of the truth about the
human condition. To begin with praise is to acknowledge this condition. Praise reflects not only the splen-
dor and power of God but his mercy as well, for his
mercy and his power are one. Thus to praise is not only
to bring God's presence to awareness but to know that
presence as care and concern.

When one says that the beginning of prayer is praise,
not petition, one is saying that what makes prayer
prayer is the complete turning of the heart to God.
Prayer demands a change of consciousness. Consciousness is ordinarily centered on the self. In prayer it is
God's goodness and power which are at the center. Our
action becomes prayer at the moment in which we
forget ourselves and become aware of God. When we
move away from or beyond the thought of personal
need to the thought of the divine grace alone, that
instant is prayer.

It is not that petition has no place in prayer, but rather that the underlying petition, if we may call it that, is the petition that God might intervene in our lives, that his will might prevail in our affairs. "We seek to submit our interests to His concern, and seek to be allied with what is ultimately right."[29] We make a mistake if we think of prayer as analogous to dialogue with other human beings or to the petitioning that takes place between humans. Prayer is not like human conversation. "We do not communicate with God. We only make ourselves communicable to Him." Prayer is not a relationship between persons, between one subject and another. Rather, in prayer we try to become "the object of His thought."[30]

At the heart of prayer, in contrast to many petitions, it is God, not the self, which is of concern. Not the self, but the surrender of self is the substance of prayer. Prayer is a way of mastering the ego. "Genuine prayer is an event in which man surpasses himself."[31] This is why Heschel speaks of prayer as an "it-He" relationship, not an I-Thou relationship.[32] He thinks the image of *immersion* is a better one for prayer than that of dialogue. We become "its" within the presence of God, immersed, touched, surrounded by the waters of mercy. The closer we come to God, the less we can speak of "I." The "I" is dust and ashes. Only God says "I." One becomes a real I by becoming known of God, by becoming worthy of being His thought. This is what prayer makes possible. It is the path toward making our existence worthy of being known to God. It is the gate to grace. "Prayer may not save us," writes Heschel, "but it makes us worthy of being saved."[33]

We transcend the self in prayer, but, as we have pointed out, this does not mean that the self is not involved. Prayer includes self-examination, self-clarification. We look at our hopes, our intentions, and try to master what is inferior in us. We attempt to make our lives compatible with God's will. Prayer is thus an act

of self-purification, a time of being honest with ourselves and with God. We try to disclose ourselves to the
sustainer of all. Heschel puts this interrelationship between self and self-surrender in another way. Prayer
consists in two inner acts. The first is an act of *turning*.
I turn away from the "I," from the concerns of the self
and from the world. The second is *direction.* "Divested
of all concerns I am overwhelmed by only one desire:
to place my heart on the altar of God."[34] Or sometimes
he speaks of prayer being primarily *kavanah*, "the
yielding of the entire being to one goal, the gathering
of the soul into focus."[35] This focusing involves the self,
for prayer is an act of sacrifice with the self replacing
the ancient animal sacrifices. But in the sacrifice of the
unfocused self, God's relation to the self comes to the
fore.

WORDS AND SILENCE

One of the distinctive elements in Heschel's understanding of prayer is the attention he gives to the significance of words. The depersonalization of the present age has brought a profanization of language. Words
have become labels, talk—double-talk. Words have lost
their power. They are regarded as functional tools. We
speak in clichés. Our words are trite. There is no sense
of the dignity of words, their creative force, their wonder and mystery. Yet, Heschel believes, words of prayer
are repositories of the spirit. For prayer to achieve its
true depth we must recover a reverence for words,
purify language, sanctify human speech.

Prayer involves a right connection between words
and persons. The renewal of language begins with the
realization that words may have a binding force and
that words of prayer are like pledges in the making.
They are commitments. We do not so much use words
as signs for things but in order to see things differently
in the light of the words. This judgment should be

related to the earlier comment that prayer involves a fundamental change in consciousness. The change comes to pass "by means of the word." "A word is a focus at which meanings meet and from which meanings seem to proceed."[36] In prayer we confront the word, face its dignity, singularity, and potential might. The meaning of this assertion becomes clearer when we see what Heschel has to say about the two forms of prayer, prayer as an act of expression and prayer as an act of empathy. Prayer as an act of expression begins with a human concern. The words follow to articulate that concern. But prayer may begin with the words. We may not be in a prayerful mood. We may have no specific concern. Through using the words of the prayer book, through feeling the words, empathizing with the ideas carried by the words, through imaginative projection of our consciousness into the meaning of the words, we may be able to rise to the greatness of prayer. The experience of prayer need not come all at once. "It grows in the face of the word that comes ever more to light in its richness, buoyancy and mystery."[37] Since words can carry and deepen such meanings, Heschel regards the words of prayer as an "island in this world." The prayer of expression may move us to thoughts that are beyond our power for expression. We may even arrive at words that are beyond our power of empathy. In either case prayer can lead us to a height and to a depth that goes beyond the words themselves. Prayer means to take hold of a word which is like a line which leads to God. But in one's praying, that word leading upward has an echo that penetrates the depth of the soul. Words in prayer are therefore to be celebrated as a holy reality. This double-edged capacity of prayer reflects a certain polarity and ambivalence about words in prayer. The word stands for more than the mind can absorb, and the mind bears more than the word can convey.

For the most part, prayer lives in words, but there is

a form of prayer that is beyond words.[38] At the highest
level of understanding, human beings are reduced to
silence. "To thee," writes the psalmist, "silence is
praise" (Ps. 65:2, Heb.; v. 1, Eng.). Heschel regards the
Jewish liturgy as a higher form of silence.

The individual is silent. He does not bring forth his own
words. His saying the consecrated words is in essence an act
of listening to what they convey. The spirit of Israel speaks.
The self is silent.[39]

And beyond both speech and silence there is song. In
some final sense, "true prayer is song."[40]

INWARDNESS AND EXTERNAL PERFORMANCE

Just as there is a polarity between what can be said
in words and what cannot be said, so too there are other
polarities involved in prayer just as there are in all
aspects of reality. Heschel lists "order and outburst,
regularity and spontaneity, uniformity and individual-
ity, law and freedom, a duty and a prerogative, empathy and self-expression, insight and sensitivity, creed
and faith, the word and that which is beyond words."[41]
We have already spoken of the contrast between empathy and self-expression. The substance of the other
polarities may be clarified by an examination of the
contrast between inwardness *(kavanah)* and external
performance.

In Judaism there is a certain tension between *hala-
cha* (law) and *agada* (inwardness), but there is also an
essential reciprocity. Tradition and freedom should interact, yet in prayer, if there is a primacy, even tradition itself insists on the primacy of *kavanah* over external performance. "Prayer without *kavanah* is no
prayer at all," declares Maimonides.[42] "Prayer without
kavanah is like a body without a soul."[43] *Kavanah,* or
inwardness, is attentiveness and awareness of what we
are saying, but it is more than this. It is "attentiveness

to God, an act of appreciation of being able to stand in the presence of God."[44] *Kavanah* requires preparation, inner purification, getting into the proper frame of mind and spirit. Such a mind and spirit is important in individual prayer, but it is particularly needed in congregational prayer. Heschel believes that prayer may often be uttered in a way or in a situation that does not encourage inner participation. A tendency toward detachment and mere outward observance must be avoided. Congregations as well as individuals must learn how to prepare for prayer so that inner participation is reached. Heschel writes: "Unless a person knows how to pray alone he is incapable of praying within the congregation. The future of congregational prayer depends on whether the Jews will learn how to pray when they are alone."[45] Heschel sees such training in developing the proper understanding, atmosphere, and capacity for prayer to be the peculiar responsibility of both the rabbi and the cantor.[46]

Heschel's insistence on the need to learn to pray does not mean that for him prayer is a matter of technique. It is not a specialized art. "All of life must be a training to pray. We pray the way we live."[47] And we live or ought to live the way we pray. Prayer should not be in conflict with the rest of our life. The divorce between liturgy and living, between prayer and practice, is, he thinks, a scandal and a disaster. A word uttered in prayer is a word of promise. It is a commitment. It goes beyond itself. For the Jew, prayer is a deed leading to actions in the world. Prayer is a *mitzvah*. A *mitzvah* is a deed in the form of a prayer. The Jewish way to God is not through speculation, nor through faith alone, but through religious acts. What this means is that there is an intimate and reciprocal relation between observance, custom, ceremonies, ethical action, and prayer. "Judaism stands and falls with the idea of the absolute relevance of human deeds. . . . *Imitatio dei* is in deeds. The deed is the source of holiness."[48] This means that worship and living are not separate. The secular and the sacred are not two different realms. Body is not apart from mind and spirit. Jews take seriously the forms of behavior even in relation to the conventional functions and amenities of life, "teaching us how to eat, how to rest, how to act."[49] "Prayer," writes Heschel, "should be part of all our ways. It does not have to be always on our lips; it must always be on our minds, in our hearts."[50] It is not that deeds save us or that we can liberate ourselves. Our hope is that God will redeem where we fail. *Mitzvoth* are ways to God. They help to sanctify man. "They confer holiness upon us, whether or not we know exactly what they signify. . . . In carrying out a mitzvah we acknowledge the fact of God being concerned with our fulfillment of His will."[51]

For the same reason prayer extends itself into worldly action. Prayer as a voice of mercy, as a cry for justice, as a plea for gentleness, moves into the world. "Prayer is private," writes Heschel, "a service of the heart; but let concern and compassion, born out of prayer, dominate public life." "Our acts must not be a refutation of our prayers."[52] Unless our deeds correspond to our prayers, we have committed an act of desecration and blasphemy.

In all prayer—whether of the individual or the community, whether related to the transformation of the individual or the community and through them of the world—our task is "to hallow time, to enable Him to enter our moments, to be at home in our time, in what we do with time." Ultimately,

prayer in Judaism is an act in the Messianic drama. We utter the words of the *Kaddish: Magnified and sanctified be His great name in the world which He has created according to His will.* Our hope is to enact, to make real the sanctification of this name here and now.[53]

We come full circle. If this is what prayer is to be, we are far from it. Our predicament is that we do not know how to pray or what to pray for. We have lost the ability to be shocked. We must pray to be shocked—at the atrocities committed by man, the Hiroshimas, the Auschwitzes, the scandal of perpetual desecration of the world. We must pray for the capacity to be dismayed at our inability to be dismayed. The world is aflame with atrocity and evil, and we are callous participants or at best indifferent onlookers. Prayer must be the place of deepening concern. It is meaningless unless it seeks to be subversive, to overthrow the callousness and hatred of our time. "The liturgical movements," says Heschel, "must become a revolutionary movement seeking to overcome the forces that continue to destroy the promise, the hope, the vision."[54]

PRAYER AS A LIGHT WITHIN US

Heschel's teaching on prayer is both original and traditional, both Jewish and universal. In interpreting his views we have not tried to keep these elements separate. Much of what he has to say about the importance of Israel and its memories, its customs and observances, is a reflection of his starting point as a Jewish theologian, but these views are set in a wider philosophical and theological context. It is the *human* situation and the *human* experience of wonder and mystery which ground the meaning of prayer in human existence. Prayer is the one universal human language. As Heschel says explicitly in a paper on the ecumenical movement:

Different are the languages of prayer, but the tears are the same. We have a vision in common of Him in whose compassion all men's prayers meet.[55]

In many theologies of prayer there is much argument and speculation about the efficacy of prayer. It is clear that for Heschel the usual discussion of such an issue is not relevant. For Heschel, to speak of God's pathos is to affirm that man's action reaches God, touches God, affects God. Prayer is the kind of action that reestablishes the relationship God claims for human beings, that of partners bringing his will and presence to bear upon the world. These changes may ultimately change the human world. They take place in the dimension of the holy. Prayer is not only a light before us; it may become a "light within us." "Those who have once been resplendent with this light find little meaning in speculations about the efficacy of prayer."[56] More than this, Heschel explicitly asserts that prayer does not "entwine itself directly with the chain of physical cause and effect; the spiritual does not interfere with the natural order of things." Men and women pray rather "from the conviction that there is a realm in which the acts of faith are puissant and potent, that there is a realm in which things of the spirit can be of momentous consequence."[57]

That prayer is central to the religious and moral life is clearly Heschel's burning conviction. It is the key also to authentic theology. "The test of authentic theology is the degree to which it reflects and enhances the power of prayer, the way of worship."[58] Prayer itself depends on that kind of knowledge which Heschel calls understanding. It both grows out of insight and has the power to generate insight. Prayer cannot live in a theological vacuum, nor can genuine theology live without prayer. Heschel clearly does not mean that prayer is derivative from conceptual knowledge. It comes out of the "awareness of the mystery of God rather than out of information about Him."[59]

Not only the theologian but the preacher also should see his task in the context of prayer. "Preaching is either an organic part of the act of prayer or out of place." "Preach in order to pray. Preach in order to inspire others to pray. The test of a true sermon is that it can be converted to prayer," says Heschel.[60]

TORN BETWEEN JOY AND ANXIETY

Toward the end of his life Rabbi Heschel turned away from writing on general philosophical and theological topics and began work on the thought and career of Reb Menachem Mendl of Kotzk, known as the Kotzker. A part of this work was published under the title *A Passion for Truth*. In his Introduction to this work, subtitled "Why I Had to Write This Book," Heschel indicates that his own personal history and thought was dominated by the polar influences drawn from the Baal Shem Tov on the one hand and from the Kotzker on the other. The Baal Shem Tov, eighteenth-century founder of the Hasidic movement, brought a radical shift in the religious outlook of Jewry. He taught that the Divine is present in everything, especially in man, and that in this world there are deeds that can affect "the worlds above." The Kotzker, a seeming descendant of the founder's line of succession in the following century, represents the opposite pole. Where the Baal Shem had emphasized love and compassion and had urged men and women to love with joy in this world, the Kotzker demanded "constant tension and unmitigated militancy in combating this worldliness."[61] Heschel regards the Kotzker as a Jewish counterpart to Kierkegaard and writes at length of the similarity between the two. Heschel sees himself as divided between opposing truths, torn between the joy taught by the Baal Shem and the anxiety of the Kotzker, the emphasis on song in the Baal Shem and on silence in the Kotzker. He writes:

The Kotzker's presence recalls the nightmare of mendacity. The presence of the Baal Shem is an assurance that falsehood dissolves into compassion through the power of love. The Baal Shem suspends sadness, the Kotzker enhances it. The Baal Shem helped me to refine my sense of immediate mystery; the Kotzker warned me of the constant peril of forfeiting authenticity.[62]

Toward the end of his life the Kotzker withdrew more and more and struggled more and more with the problem of evil, with Job's problem. In reading Heschel one feels that in dealing with the horrors of Auschwitz; with the mistreatment and injustice toward blacks, the aged, and children; with the problems of Vietnam, and with the lies, duplicity, and callousness of contemporary life, he like the Kotzker was wrestling with God. It is all the more important, then, to grasp what Heschel says about prayer. He writes: "Life in our time has been a nightmare for many of us, tranquillity an interlude, happiness a fake. . . . The agony of our problem foments like a volcano, and it is foolish to seek finite answers to infinite agony. . . . The pain is strong as death, cruel as the grave." Yet: "At times we must believe in Him in spite of Him, to continue being a witness despite His hiding Himself. What experience fails to convey, prayer brings about. Prayer prevails over despair."[63] Heschel then tells the following story about a friend's experience. It might be a commentary on his own view of prayer and on his statement: "Faith is the beginning of compassion, compassion for God. It is when bursting with God's sighs that we are touched by the awareness that *beyond all absurdity* there is meaning, Truth, and love."

A friend of mine, Mr. Sh. Z. Shragai, went to Poland as a representative of the Jewish Agency in the late 1940's, when Poland still entertained good relations with the state of Israel. His visit was an official mission concerning the emigration of Jewish survivors of Nazi extermination camps. After finishing his work in Warsaw, he left for Paris and, as a very important person, was given a whole compartment on the train. It was crowded with passengers.

Outside he noticed an emaciated, poorly clad Jew who could not find a seat on the train. He invited him to join him in his compartment. It was comfortable, clean, pleasant, and the poor fellow came in with his bundle, put it on the rack over the seat, and sat down.

My friend tried to engage him in conversation, but he would not talk. When evening came, my friend, an observing Jew, recited the evening prayer *(maariv)*, while the other fellow did not say a word of prayer. The following morning my friend took out his prayer shawl and phylacteries *(Talit and Tefillin)* and said his prayer; the other fellow, who looked so wretched and somber, would not say a word and did not pray.

Finally, when the day was almost over, they started a conversation. The fellow said, "I am never going to pray any more because of what happened to us in Auschwitz. . . . How could I pray? That is why I did not pray all day."

The following morning—it was a long trip from Warsaw to Paris—my friend noticed that the fellow suddenly opened his bundle, took out his *Talit* and *Tefillin* and started to pray. He asked him afterward, "What made you change your mind?"

The fellow said, "It suddenly dawned upon me to think how lonely God must be; look with whom He is left. I felt sorry for Him."[64]

Afterword:
Issues and Questions

THE MOST STRIKING CONCLUSION from the studies of the theology of prayer presented in this book is that the creative theologians of our time, in contrast to their nineteenth-century predecessors with the exception of Kierkegaard, have taken the problem of prayer with utmost seriousness. Equally striking is the diversity of their interpretations. While part of that diversity is rooted in different assessments of the nature and task of a theology of prayer and of theology itself, a significant part of it is derived from the divergent approaches to what has become in our day the central issue in a theology of prayer. As Heschel said, the issue of prayer is not prayer but God, and the major difficulties contemporaries have with prayer cluster around the God question. The critical issue in a theology of prayer is what is to be said about God and God's relation to human existence. The issue is both methodological and substantive.

The theologies studied in this book differ in basic ways both in their views concerning how the God question is to be approached and in the resources they believe should be used in responding to it. Can one rest one's case on a confessional position, on tradition, on biblical revelation, or on religious experience? Can the resources of philosophy (be it existentialist, process, phenomenology, language analysis, or some other) and the human sciences profitably be used in relation to the problem of God and the meaning of prayer? The answers to these methodological questions have serious consequences for the fundamental conceptuality that the various theologians will use for speaking of God. God is a personal being. God is not a personal being. God is Being itself. God is the creative good. God is Presence. God is ultimate mystery, beyond the grasp of human language. God is unchanging. God undergoes change. God is all powerful. God's power is limited. God enters into dialogue. God does not enter into dialogue. A similar pluralism and diversity appears if we compare the ways God is said to be related to human freedom and to causal process in nature and history. Such pluralism raises critical questions about the meaning and cognitive status of religious language and theological statements. This issue is important not only in relation to prayer as a language and to the language of prayer but also in relation to the problem of God and God's responsiveness to prayer.

Other theological issues about the meaning of prayer appear to be related to, if not derivative from, those clustering around the question of God and God's relationship to human existence. We shall state some of them briefly in the form of direct questions.

1. How is prayer related to what Christians have called the Christ and to what they have called the Spirit? This issue is of critical importance because claims have made about both Christ and the Spirit that either deny relationship or provide a way of relating Christian prayer to prayer in non-Christian religions or among those who would claim no religion at all.

2. How are solitary and communal prayer related to each other and to the being and nurture of the community in which they take place? These questions highlight the social dimension of prayer and the social dimensions of human existence itself.

3. If what the theologian says about God is central for the interpretation of prayer, the understanding of

human existence is hardly less so. If we really know what the reality of God is, we will know what authentic human existence is. If we really understand what human existence is, we will understand what God is. Putting the theological question about human being and becoming in the simplest way, we can ask: What is wrong? How and why is human existence filled with suffering, evil, brokenness? What is the goal of human life? What does it mean to be fully human? What would it mean to overcome the brokenness and distortion of human life? How do the individual and the community move in the direction of such becoming and away from their present condition? How is prayer related to the answers to these questions?

4. Human existence has not only a present and a past but a future. The future enters into the life of the individual and the community either as hope and expectation or as anxiety and fear. What is the relation of prayer to the future? To the human vision of what might be? To the hope that gives direction and courage or the dread that may fill the mind and spirit as one contemplates death or catastrophe? In traditional terms one might speak of this as the question of the relationship between prayer and what Christians and Jews have called the Kingdom of God. Not many of the theologians we have discussed have dealt explicitly with this issue in their theologies of prayer. Some have been more aware of the relevance of prayer to the human social predicament than others, but the eschatological dimensions of prayer have not been clearly delineated.

There is a new situation in the contemporary world. The growing awareness of injustice and oppression have given rise to liberation movements and political and liberation theologies. There is a new vision of the possibility of freedom, equality, and justice spreading across the face of the world. It is present in the black liberation movements, in the women's movement, in the struggle against oppression in Latin America and elsewhere. At the same time, the forces of class domination and oppression resist and struggle against change. For many who draw their vision from religious faith the problem of prayer is no longer a question of a balance between contemplation and action, but rather one of the direct relevance of prayer to political, social, and economic change. This question is posed in two ways. Is traditional prayer and piety a means of escape and an ideologically grounded way of maintaining oppression? Is prayer only, as Moltmann says it is for many, "an inner tranquillizing of the self or a religious flight from the world," or can and ought prayer to be integrally tied to liberating action in the political struggle?[1]

When the question of prayer and action is posed in this fashion, the relation of God to the world is seen in a new way. Such issues are not only eschatological, that is, questions about the future and the future of God, but they are questions that may dominate the future of the theology of prayer. The future of the theology of prayer is tied to living religious faith. So long as there is an awareness of a reality which transcends the human, and a sense that that reality is responsive to human need and human action, there will be prayer and there will be theology of prayer, as men and women try to understand how to respond to the one who responds to them.

Notes

Chapter 1

HISTORICAL BACKGROUND

1. Fernand Ménégoz, *Le Problème de la Prière* (Libraire Istra, 1925).

2. Paul Tillich, *Perspectives on 19th and 20th Century Protestant Theology,* ed. by Carl E. Braaten (Harper & Row, 1967), p. 64.

3. Immanuel Kant, *Religion Within the Limits of Reason Alone,* tr. and with an introduction and notes by Theodore M. Greene and Hoyt H. Hudson (Harper & Row, Harper Torchbooks, 1960), p. 180

4. Ibid., p. 181.

5. Ibid., p. 183.

6. Ibid.

7. Ibid., pp. 184–185.

8. Ibid.

9. Quoted by Allen W. Wood, *Kant's Moral Religion* (Cornell University Press, 1970), p. 162.

10. Friedrich Schleiermacher, *The Christian Faith,* ed. by H. R. Macintosh and J. S. Stewart (Harper & Row, 1963), Vol. II, p. 672.

11. Ibid., Vol. II, p. 669.

12. Ibid.

13. Ibid., p. 671.

14. Ibid., p. 672.

15. Ibid.

16. Ibid., p. 673.

17. Ibid.

18. Ibid.

19. Friedrich Schleiermacher, *Selected Sermons,* tr. by Mary F. Wilson (London: Hodder & Stoughton, 1890), p. 38.

20. Ibid., p. 40.

21. Ibid., p. 43.

22. Ibid., p. 45.

23. Ibid.

24. Ibid., p. 46.

25. The quotations under *(a)* thru *(c)* are drawn from ibid., pp. 47–50.

26. Ibid., pp. 43–44.

27. Ibid., p. 674.

28. Ludwig Feuerbach, *The Essence of Christianity,* tr. by George Eliot (Harper & Row, Harper Torchbooks, 1957), p. 121.

29. Ibid., p. 122.

30. Ibid.

31. Ibid., p. 123.

32. Ibid., p. 125.

33. Quoted from Ritschl in David L. Mueller, *An Introduction to the Theology of Albrecht Ritschl* (Westminster Press, 1969), p. 122.

34. Albrecht Ritschl, *The Christian Doctrine of Justification and Reconciliation: The Positive Development of the Doctrine,* tr. by H. R. Mackintosh and A. B. Macaulay (Scribners, 1900), Vol. III, p. 457.

35. Albrecht Ritschl, *Three Essays,* tr. by Philip Hefner (Fortress Press, 1972), p. 255. (The third essay is Ritschl's "Instruction.")

36. Ritschl, *Justification and Reconciliation,* p. 642.

37. Ibid.

38. Ibid., p. 646.

39. Ibid., p. 641.

40. Ibid., p. 644.

41. Ibid.

42. Ibid.

43. Ibid.

44. Wilhelm Herrmann, *The Communion of the Christian with God,* tr. by J. Sandys Sanyon (G. P. Putnam's Sons, 1913), p. 202.

45. Ibid., p. 203.

46. Ibid., p. 205.

47. Ibid.

48. Ibid., pp. 331–332.

49. Ibid., p. 332.

50. Ibid., p. 333.

51. Wilhelm Herrmann, art. "Prayer," in *The New Schaff-*

Herzog Encyclopedia of Religious Knowledge, ed. by S. M. Jackson (Funk & Wagnalls Co., 1911). Vol. IX, p. 155.

52. Herrmann, *The Communion of the Christian with God,* p. 334.

53. Ibid., p. 335.

54. Ibid., p. 337.

55. Ibid., p. 338.

56. Ibid., p. 339.

57. Ibid.

58. Ibid., p. 341.

59. Herrmann, art. "Prayer," loc. cit., p. 156.

60. Ibid.

61. Ibid.

62. Ibid.

63. Perry LeFevre, *The Prayers of Kierkegaard* (University of Chicago Press, 1956).

Chapter 2

KARL BARTH

1. Karl Barth, *God, Grace, and Gospel,* ed. by T. F. Torrance and J. K. S. Reid (*Scottish Journal of Theology* Occasional Papers, No. 5, 1957), p. 57.

2. Karl Barth, *The Word of God and the Word of Man,* tr. by Douglas Horton (Pilgrim Press, 1928), pp. 104–106.

3. Ibid., p. 43.

4. Quoted by D. F. Ford in *Karl Barth: Studies in His Theological Method,* ed. by S. W. Sykes (Oxford University Press, 1979), p. 55.

5. Ostensibly an analysis and interpretation of the Reformers' views of prayer, Barth's *Prayer: According to the Catechisms of the Reformation* (note 7, below) clearly presents views consonant with his own. Only in relation to the Reformers' failure to express a fully eschatological perspective on prayer does Barth himself offer a corrective.

6. Because prayer is Christian *action,* Barth can treat it extensively in *Church Dogmatics,* Vol. III, Pt. 4, in the context of his discussion of Christian ethics.

7. Cf. Karl Barth, *Prayer: According to the Catechisms of the Reformation* (Westminster Press, 1952), pp. 17–19.

8. Karl Barth, *Church Dogmatics,* III/3, p. 268.

9. Barth, *Prayer,* p. 21.

10. Barth, *Church Dogmatics,* III/3, p. 283.

11. Barth, *Prayer,* p. 34.

12. Ibid.

13. Ibid., p. 23.

14. Barth, *Church Dogmatics,* III/3, p. 285.

15. Ibid., p. 288.

16. Ibid., III/4, p. 87.

17. Barth, *Prayer,* p. 39.

18. Ibid., p. 57.

19. Ibid., p. 26.

20. Karl Barth, *The Epistle to the Romans,* tr. from the 6th ed. by Edwyn C. Hoskyns (Oxford University Press, 1933), pp. 316–317.

21. Barth, *Church Dogmatics,* III/4, p. 90.

22. Barth, *Prayer,* p. 27.

23. Barth, *Church Dogmatics,* III/4, p. 90.

24. Ibid., p. 97.

25. Barth, *Church Dogmatics,* IV/2, p. 704.

26. Ibid., p. 705.

27. Barth, *Church Dogmatics,* III/4, p. 106.

28. Barth, *Prayer,* p. 21.

29. Ibid., p. 23.

30. Barth, *Church Dogmatics,* III/4, p. 109.

31. Ibid., p. 101.

32. Barth, *Prayer,* p. 38.

33. Ibid., p. 41.

34. Ibid., p. 45.

35. Ibid., p. 49.

36. Ibid., p. 55.

37. Karl Barth, *Anselm: Fides Quaerens Intellectum* (John Knox Press, 1958), p. 11.

38. Ibid., p. 40.

39. Karl Barth, *Evangelical Theology: An Introduction* (Holt, Rinehart & Winston, 1963), p. 160.

40. Ibid.

41. Ibid., p. 168.

42. Ibid., p. 167.

43. Ibid., p. 160.

44. Ibid., pp. 169–170.

Chapter 3

HENRY NELSON WIEMAN

1. Quoted by William S. Minor in *Creativity in Henry Nelson Wieman* (Scarecrow Press, 1977), p. xvii.

2. Henry Nelson Wieman, *Religious Experience and the Scientific Method* (Macmillan Co., 1926), p. 15.

3. Ibid., p. 38.
4. Ibid., p. 39.
5. Ibid., p. 74.
6. Ibid., p. 84.
7. Henry Nelson Wieman, *The Wrestle of Religion with Truth* (Macmillan Co., 1928), p. vi.
8. Ibid., p. 69.
9. Ibid., pp. 71–72.
10. Ibid., p. 73.
11. Ibid.
12. Ibid., p. 76.
13. Henry Nelson Wieman, *The Issues of Life* (Abingdon-Cokesbury Press, 1930), pp. 162–163.
14. Ibid., p. 225.
15. Ibid., p. 231.
16. Ibid., p. 235.
17. Ibid.
18. Ibid., p. 237.
19. Henry Nelson Wieman and Regina H. Wieman, *Normative Psychology of Religion* (Thomas Y. Crowell Co., 1935), p. 130.
20. Ibid., p. 136.
21. Ibid., p. 137.
22. Ibid.
23. Ibid., p. 140.
24. Henry Nelson Wieman, *The Source of Human Good* (University of Chicago Press, 1946), p. 56.
25. Ibid., p. 58.
26. Ibid., p. 282.
27. Ibid.
28. Henry Nelson Wieman, *Man's Ultimate Commitment* (Southern Illinois University Press, 1958), p. 12.
29. Ibid., p. 17.
30. Ibid., p. 5. Cf. also p. 37.
31. Wieman, *The Source of Human Good,* p. 41.
32. Ibid., p. 44.
33. Henry Nelson Wieman, *Methods of Private Religious Living* (Macmillan Co., 1929), p. 5.
34. Ibid., p. 18.
35. Ibid., p. 21.
36. Ibid., p. 23.
37. Ibid., pp. 30–33.
38. Wieman and Wieman, *Normative Psychology of Religion,* p. 146.

Chapter 4

PAUL TILLICH

1. From Paul Tillich, "God as Reality and Symbol," cited by Carl J. Armbruster in *The Vision of Paul Tillich* (Sheed & Ward, 1967), p. 152.

2. Paul Tillich, *Systematic Theology,* Vol. III (University of Chicago Press, 1963), p. 192.

3. Ibid., p. 18.

4. Ibid., p. 120.

5. Ibid.

6. *Systematic Theology,* Vol. I (University of Chicago Press, 1951), p. 127.

7. Ibid.

8. *Systematic Theology,* Vol. III, p. 190.

9. Ibid., p. 191.

10. Ibid., p. 111.

11. Ibid.

12. Ibid., p. 129.

13. Ibid.

14. Ibid., p. 192.

15. Ibid., p. 31.

16. *Systematic Theology,* Vol. I, p. 266.

17. Ibid., p. 267.

18. Ibid.

19. Paul Tillich, *The Shaking of the Foundations* (Charles Scribner's Sons, 1948), p. 139.

20. *Systematic Theology,* Vol. I, p. 289.

21. Paul Tillich, *What Is Religion?* ed. by James Luther Adams (Harper & Row, 1969), p. 59.

22. Ibid., p. 82.

23. Ibid., p. 147.

24. *Systematic Theology,* Vol. I, p. 224.

25. Paul Tillich, *Christianity and the Encounter of the World Religions* (Columbia University Press, 1963), p. 67.

26. Ibid., p. 81.

27. Ibid., p. 82.

Chapter 5

DIETRICH BONHOEFFER

1. Dietrich Bonhoeffer, *The Communion of Saints* (1930; Harper & Row, 1963), p. 122.

2. Ibid., p. 125.

3. Ibid., p. 130.

4. Ibid., p. 132.

5. Ibid.

6. Ibid., p. 133.

7. Ibid.

8. Ibid.

9. Ibid., p. 134.

10. Ibid.

11. Eberhard Bethge, *Dietrich Bonhoeffer* (Harper & Row, 1970), p. 335.

12. Dietrich Bonhoeffer, *The Way to Freedom,* ed. by Edwin H. Robertson (Harper & Row, 1966), p. 117.

13. Ibid.

14. Ibid., p. 118.

15. Bethge, *Dietrich Bonhoeffer,* p. 385.

16. Dietrich Bonhoeffer, *Life Together* (Harper & Row, 1954), pp. 36–37.

17. Ibid., p. 17.

18. Ibid., p. 20.

19. Ibid., pp. 45–46.

20. Ibid., p. 47.

21. Ibid., p. 49.

22. Ibid., p. 50.

23. Dietrich Bonhoeffer, *Psalms: The Prayer Book of the Bible* (Augsburg Publishing House, 1970), p. 11.

24. Ibid., p. 14.

25. Bonhoeffer, *Life Together,* p. 53.

26. Ibid., p. 57.

27. Ibid., p. 61.

28. Ibid., p. 65.

29. Ibid., p. 71.

30. Ibid., p. 73.

31. Ibid., p. 74.

32. Bethge, *Dietrich Bonhoeffer,* p. 386.

33. Bonhoeffer, *Life Together,* pp. 84–85.

34. Ibid., p. 86.

35. Ibid.

36. Ibid., p. 88.

37. Ibid., p. 89.

38. Wolf-Dieter Zimmermann and Ronald Gregor Smith (eds.), *I Knew Dietrich Bonhoeffer* (Harper & Row, 1967), pp. 108–110.

39. Bethge, *Dietrich Bonhoeffer,* p. 380.

40. Dietrich Bonhoeffer, *The Cost of Discipleship* (1937; Macmillan Co., 1938), p. 56.

41. Ibid., p. 129.
42. Ibid., p. 131.
43. Ibid., p. 161.
44. Ibid., p. 140.
45. Dietrich Bonhoeffer, *Letters and Papers from Prison,* enlarged edition (Macmillan Co., 1972), p. 369 (21 July 1944).
46. Ibid., p. 360 (16 July).
47. Ibid., p. 281 (30 April).
48. Ibid., pp. 279–280 (30 April).
49. Ibid., p. 286 (5 May).
50. Ibid., p. 281 (30 April).
51. Ibid., p. 300.
52. Bethge, *Dietrich Bonhoeffer,* p. 788.
53. Ibid., p. 784, n. 237.
54. Zimmermann and Smith (eds.), *I Knew Dietrich Bonhoeffer,* p. 232.

Chapter 6

C. S. LEWIS

1. C. S. Lewis, *Letters to Malcolm: Chiefly on Prayer* (Harcourt, Brace and World, 1964), p. 55.
2. Ibid., p. 21.
3. Ibid., p. 56.
4. Ibid., p. 78.
5. Ibid., p. 79.
6. Ibid., p. 80.
7. Ibid., p. 81.
8. Ibid., p. 82.
9. Ibid., p. 37.
10. Ibid., p. 55.
11. Cf. C. S. Lewis, *The Screwtape Letters* (Macmillan Co., 1943), pp. 138–140, where Lewis has Screwtape giving Wormwood advice on stirring up the believer about such theological puzzles.
12. Lewis, *Letters to Malcolm,* p. 49.
13. Ibid., p. 50.
14. C. S. Lewis, *Undeceptions,* ed. by Walter Hooper (London: Geoffrey Bles, 1971), p. 79, in the essay "Work and Prayer."
15. Ibid.
16. C. S. Lewis, *The World's Last Night* (Harcourt, Brace and Co., 1960), p. 10, in the essay "The Efficacy of Prayer."
17. *Letters of C. S. Lewis,* ed. by W. H. Lewis (London: Geoffrey Bles, 1966), p. 236.

18. Lewis, *Letters to Malcolm,* p. 50.
19. Ibid.
20. Ibid., p. 57.
21. Ibid., p. 61.
22. Ibid.
23. Ibid.
24. Lewis, *Screwtape Letters,* p. 137.
25. Lewis, *The World's Last Night,* p. 8.
26. Ibid.
27. Lewis, *Letters to Malcolm,* p. 34.
28. Ibid., p. 99.
29. Ibid.
30. Ibid., p. 89.
31. Ibid., p. 90.
32. Ibid., pp. 92–93.
33. Ibid., p. 74.
34. Ibid.
35. Ibid., p. 69.
36. Ibid., p. 75.
37. Ibid., p. 69.
38. Cf., e.g., James T. Como (ed.), *C. S. Lewis at the Breakfast Table* (Macmillan Publishing Co., 1979), p. 232, and W.
H. Lewis (ed.), *Letters of C. S. Lewis,* p. 300.
39. Lewis, *Letters to Malcolm,* p. 15.
40. Ibid., p. 16.
41. Como (ed.), *C. S. Lewis at the Breakfast Table,* pp. 199,
205, 232.
42. Lewis, *The Screwtape Letters,* pp. 26–28.
43. Lewis, *Letters to Malcolm,* p. 116.
44. W. H. Lewis (ed.), *Letters of C. S. Lewis,* p. 147.

Chapter 7

THOMAS MERTON

1. Thomas Merton, *Spiritual Direction and Meditation;
and, What Is Contemplation?* (Anthony Clarke Books, 1975),
p. 96.
2. Ibid., p. 98.
3. Ibid., p. 95.
4. Ibid., p. 97. Merton wrote more about these "hidden
contemplatives" who find God through action. He says that
they, "far from being excluded from perfection, may reach
a higher degree of sanctity than others" who have a deeper
interior life. "These men live for God and for His love alone,"
writes Merton. Cf. Raymond Bailey, *Thomas Merton on Mys-*

ticism (Doubleday & Co., Image Books, 1976), p. 160. Bailey quotes from Merton's unpublished "Inner Experience," pp. 62–63.

5. Merton, "Inner Experience," p. 6, quoted in Bailey, op. cit., p. 162.

6. Merton, "Inner Experience," p. 35; quoted in Bailey, op. cit., pp. 161–162.

7. Merton, "Inner Experience," p. 88; quoted in Bailey, op. cit., p. 176.

8. Thomas Merton, *Contemplative Prayer* (Herder & Herder, 1969), p. 34.

9. Ibid., p. 103.

10. Cf. John J. Higgins, *Thomas Merton on Prayer* (Doubleday & Co., Image Books, 1975), pp. 58–63.

11. Merton, *Contemplative Prayer,* p. 33.

12. Ibid., p. 38.

13. Ibid., p. 35.

14. Ibid., p. 39.

15. Ibid.

16. Ibid., p. 40.

17. Ibid., pp. 48–49.

18. Merton, "Inner Experience," pp. 77–78; quoted in Bailey, op. cit., p. 164.

19. Merton, *Contemplative Prayer,* p. 53.

20. Ibid., p. 54.

21. Ibid., p. 83.

22. Ibid., p. 86.

23. Ibid., p. 87.

24. Ibid., p. 95.

25. Ibid., p. 96.

26. Ibid., p. 97.

27. Ibid.

28. Ibid.

29. Ibid., p. 99.

30. Ibid., p. 102.

31. Ibid., pp. 103–104.

32. Ibid., p. 111.

33. Merton, *Spiritual Direction,* p. 102.

34. Parallel forms of this material are to be found in Merton, *Spiritual Direction,* p. 103, and "Inner Experience," p. 184 (quoted in Bailey, op. cit., p. 174). There are minor variants.

35. Merton, *Spiritual Direction,* p. 62.

36. Ibid., p. 71.

37. Ibid., p. 74.

38. Ibid., p. 76.

39. Ibid., p. 77.

40. Ibid., p. 80.

41. Merton, *Contemplative Prayer,* p. 50. Cf. also p. 33.

42. Much could be written about Merton's understanding of silence. Cf. Merton, *Contemplative Prayer,* p. 33; John F. Teahan, "Thomas Merton's Spirituality," *American Benedictine Review,* Vol. 30, No. 2 (June 1979); and P. J. Kountz's doctoral dissertation at the University of Chicago (1976) entitled "Thomas Merton as Writer and Monk."

43. Cf. Teahan, "Thomas Merton's Spirituality," loc. cit., pp. 114ff.

44. Merton, *Contemplative Prayer,* pp. 142–143.

45. Thomas Merton, "Contemplation in the World of Action," *Sisters Today,* Vol. 42, No. 7 (March 1971), p. 349.

46. Merton, *Spiritual Direction,* p. 96.

47. Merton, *Contemplative Prayer,* p. 55.

48. Thomas Merton, *The Sign of Jonas* (Doubleday & Co., Image Books, 1956), p. 37.

49. Teahan, "Thomas Merton's Spirituality," loc. cit., pp. 119ff.

50. Thomas Merton, "Prayer, Personalism, and the Spirit," *Sisters Today,* Vol. 42, No. 3 (Nov. 1970), p. 134.

51. Thomas Merton, "Prayer and Conscience," *Sisters Today,* Vol. 42, No. 8 (April 1971), pp. 412–413.

52. Thomas Merton, *Opening the Bible,* p. 74; quoted in Bailey, op. cit., p. 155.

53. Thomas Merton, "A Conference on Prayer," *Sisters Today,* Vol. 41, No. 8 (April 1970), p. 450.

54. Thomas Merton, *Contemplation in a World of Action* (Doubleday & Co., 1971), p. 7.

55. Ibid., p. 374.

56. Ibid., p. 332.

57. Ibid., p. 336.

58. Ibid., p. 341.

59. Merton, *Contemplative Prayer,* p. 106.

60. Thomas Merton, *The Asian Journal of Thomas Merton,* ed. by Naomi Burton et al. (New Directions Publishing Corp., 1973), p. 313.

61. Thomas Merton, *Mystics and Zen Masters* (1967; Dell Publishing Co., 1969), p. ix.

62. Thomas Merton, *Zen and the Birds of Appetite* (New Directions Publishing Corp., 1968), p. 46.

63. Merton, *Mystics and Zen Masters,* p. 209.

64. Merton, *Zen and the Birds of Appetite,* pp. 57–58.

65. Merton, *Mystics and Zen Masters,* p. viii.

66. Ibid., p. 41.

67. Ibid., p. 33.

68. Ibid., p. 253.

69. Merton, *Zen and the Birds of Appetite,* pp. 24–25.

70. Ibid., p. 25. Cf. also Thomas Merton, "The Self of Modern Man and the New Christian Consciousness," *R. M. Bucke Memorial Society Newsletter,* Vol. 2 (April 1967), p. 18.

71. Merton, *Zen and the Birds of Appetite,* p. 62.

72. Ibid., p. 24.

73. Merton, "Contemplation in the World of Action," loc. cit., p. 351. Cf. also Thomas Merton, "A New Christian Consciousness," *Theoria to Theory,* Vol. 3 (Jan. 1969), pp. 5–8.

74. Thomas Merton, "Final Integration Towards a 'Monastic Therapy,' " *Monastic Studies,* Vol. 6 (1968), p. 93.

75. Ibid., p. 94.

76. Merton, "A New Christian Consciousness," loc. cit., p. 8.

Chapter 8

KARL RAHNER

1. Karl Rahner, *Happiness Through Prayer* (Dublin: Clonmore & Reynolds, 1958), p. 8.

2. Karl Rahner, *Opportunities for Faith* (Seabury Press, 1974), p. 63, in the lecture "On Prayer Today."

3. Ibid.

4. Ibid., p. 64.

5. Ibid., p. 63.

6. Karl Rahner, *Christian at the Crossroads* (Seabury Press, 1976), p. 48, in the chapter "The Possibility and Necessity of Prayer."

7. Rahner, *Happiness Through Prayer,* p. 46.

8. Ibid., p. 57.

9. Ibid.

10. Karl Rahner, *Encounters with Silence* (Newman Press, 1960), p. 19.

11. Ibid., p. 21.

12. Ibid., p. 23.

13. Ibid.

14. Ibid.

15. Ibid., p. 24.

16. Ibid., p. 25.

17. Rahner, *Happiness Through Prayer,* p. 112.

18. Ibid., p. 14.

19. Karl Rahner, *Theological Investigations,* Vol. III, *The Theology of the Spiritual Life* (Helicon Press, 1967), p. 214, in "The Apostolate of Prayer."

20. Rahner, *Happiness Through Prayer,* p. 15.

21. Karl Rahner, *Theological Investigations,* Vol. V, *Later Writings* (Helicon Press, 1966), p. 419, in "Some Theses on Prayer in the Name of the Church."

22. Karl Rahner, *Foundations of Christian Faith: An Introduction to the Idea of Christianity* (Seabury Press, 1978), p. 21. Leo J. O'Donovan (ed.), *A World of Grace: An Introduction to the Themes and Foundations of Karl Rahner's Theology* (Seabury Press, 1980) contains relatively simple summaries of the chapters of *Foundations of Christian Faith* and suggests the most important references in Rahner's works for further reading.

23. Rahner, *Christian at the Crossroads,* pp. 60–61.

24. Ibid., p. 53.

25. Ibid.

26. Ibid., pp. 49–50.

27. Ibid., pp. 62–63.

28. Ibid., p. 66.

29. Ibid.

30. Ibid.

31. Cf. Karl-Heinz Weger, *Karl Rahner: An Introduction to His Theology* (Seabury Press, 1980), pp. 73–79.

32. Rahner, *Christian at the Crossroads,* pp. 37–38.

33. Rahner, *Foundations of Christian Faith,* pp. 88–89.

34. Ibid., pp. 71ff.

35. Rahner, *Faith and Prayer,* pp. 64–65.

36. Ibid., p. 67.

37. Ibid., p. 68.

38. Rahner, *Happiness Through Prayer,* p. 24.

39. Ibid., p. 28.

40. Ibid., p. 29.

41. Rahner, *Theological Investigations,* Vol. V, p. 419.

42. Ibid., p. 422.

43. Weger, *Karl Rahner,* p. 107.

44. Rahner, *Theological Investigations,* Vol. V, p. 425.

45. Ibid., p. 426.

46. Rahner, *Opportunities for Faith,* pp. 56, 60–61, in "Theses on the Theme Faith and Prayer."

47. Rahner, *Theological Investigations,* Vol. III, p. 219.

48. Rahner, *Opportunities for Faith,* p. 69.

49. Ibid.

50. Rahner, *Happiness Through Prayer,* p. 60.

51. Ibid., p. 65.
52. Ibid., p. 67.
53. Rahner, *Christians at the Crossroads,* p. 57.
54. Ibid., p. 58.
55. Ibid.
56. Rahner, *Opportunities for Faith,* p. 55.
57. Ibid., p. 56.
58. Ibid., p. 59.
59. Rahner, *Theological Investigations,* Vol. III, p. 226, in "A Spiritual Dialogue at Evening: On Sleep, Prayer, and Other Subjects."
60. Ibid., p. 229.
61. Ibid., p. 230.
62. Ibid.
63. Ibid., p. 231.
64. Ibid.
65. Ibid., p. 232.
66. Ibid.
67. Ibid., p. 233.
68. Ibid., p. 234.
69. Ibid., p. 235.

Chapter 9

ABRAHAM J. HESCHEL

1. Certainly this is true for Judaism, where much of the contemporary discussion of prayer focuses on the tradition rather than on the rethinking of the meaning of prayer for the contemporary situation. Cf. Jakob J. Petuchowski, *Understanding Jewish Prayer* (KTAV Publishing House, 1972); Bernard Martin, *Prayer in Judaism* (Basic Books, 1968); Louis Jacobs, *Jewish Prayer* (Jewish Chronicle Publications, 1962).
2. Abraham J. Heschel, *Man's Quest for God* (Charles Scribner's Sons, 1954), p. 87.
3. *Between God and Man: From the Writings of Abraham J. Heschel,* ed. by Fritz A. Rothschild (Harper & Bros., 1959), p. 255.
4. Abraham J. Heschel, *The Insecurity of Freedom* (Farrar, Straus & Giroux, 1966), p. 70.
5. Ibid., p. 88.
6. Ibid., p. 37.
7. Abraham J. Heschel, *God in Search of Man* (1956; Meridian Books, 1959), p. 58.
8. Ibid., p. 66.

9. Abraham J. Heschel, *Man Is Not Alone* (Farrar, Straus, & Young, 1951), pp. 68–69.

10. Heschel, *God in Search of Man,* p. 82.

11. Ibid., pp. 162–163.

12. Heschel, *Man's Quest for God,* p. 8.

13. Ibid., p. 112.

14. Heschel, *God in Search of Man,* p. 129.

15. William E. Kaufman (ed.), *Contemporary Jewish Philosophies* (Reconstructionist Press, 1976), p. 157.

16. Heschel, *Between God and Man,* p. 69.

17. Heschel, *Man Is Not Alone,* p. 109.

18. Ibid., p. 153.

19. Heschel, *Between God and Man,* p. 24.

20. Heschel, *The Insecurity of Freedom,* p. 258.

21. Heschel, *Man's Quest for God,* p. 15.

22. Ibid., p. 10.

23. Abraham J. Heschel, "On Prayer," *Conservative Judaism,* Vol. XXV, No. 1 (Fall 1970), p. 5.

24. Ibid., p. 3.

25. Ibid., p. 4.

26. Ibid.

27. Heschel, *Man's Quest for God,* p. 89.

28. Heschel, "On Prayer," loc. cit., p. 7.

29. Heschel, *Man's Quest for God,* p. 16.

30. Ibid., p. 10.

31. Ibid., p. 29.

32. Heschel, *The Insecurity of Freedom,* p. 355.

33. Ibid., p. 256.

34. Heschel, "On Prayer," loc. cit., p. 3.

35. Heschel, *Man's Quest for God,* p. 15.

36. Ibid., p. 26.

37. Ibid., p. 28.

38. Heschel, *The Insecurity of Freedom,* p. 260.

39. Heschel, *Man's Quest for God,* p. 44.

40. Ibid.

41. Ibid., p. 65.

42. Ibid., p. 66.

43. Ibid., p. 84.

44. Ibid.

45. Heschel, *The Insecurity of Freedom,* p. 215.

46. Ibid. Cf. the whole essay, "The Vocation of the Cantor."

47. Ibid., pp. 260ff.

48. Heschel, *Man's Quest for God,* p. 109.

49. Ibid.

50. Heschel, *God in Search of Man,* p. 375.

51. Heschel, *Man's Quest for God,* p. 114.
52. Heschel, "On Prayer," loc. cit., p. 5.
53. Ibid., p. 4.
54. Ibid., p. 7.
55. Heschel, *The Insecurity of Freedom,* p. 180.
56. Heschel, *Man's Quest for God,* p. 8.
57. Heschel, *Man Is Not Alone,* p. 239.
58. Heschel, "On Prayer," loc. cit., p. 1.
59. Heschel, *Man's Quest for God,* p. 88.
60. Ibid., p. 80.
61. Abraham J. Heschel, *A Passion for Truth* (Farrar Straus & Giroux, 1973), p. 10.
62. Ibid., p. xv.
63. Ibid., p. 302.
64. Ibid., pp. 302–303.

Afterword

1. Jürgen Moltmann, *The Church in the Power of the Spirit* (Harper & Row, 1977), p. 285.